MANY MANSIONS
Glimpses of Heaven

T0167007

First published by O-Books, 2013
O-Books is an imprint of John Hunt Publishing Ltd., Laurel House,
Station Approach,
Alresford, Hants, SO24 9JH, UK
office1@jhpbooks.net
www.johnhuntpublishing.com

For distributor details and how to order please visit the 'Ordering'
section on our website.

Text copyright: John Woolley 2008

ISBN: 978 1 78279 191 1

A CIP catalogue record for this book is available from the British Library.

Scripture quotations are taken from various translations.

Typesetting by New Life Publishing.

Printed in the USA by Edwards Brothers Malloy

a sequel to

I Am With You
Abide in My Love
My Burden Is Light

MANY MANSIONS
Glimpses of Heaven

treasured words of divine
inspiration as given to

Fr. John Woolley

BOOKS

Winchester, UK
Washington, USA

I dedicate *Many Mansions*
to my dear family:

Edna
Sally
Elizabeth
and Peter
(who gave us the title)

I am deeply appreciative of the
friendship and understanding of
Toni and Gerard at New Life
Publishing/Goodnews Books in
producing our book.

In the love of our Lord

John A. Woolley

I know that our Lord will speak to you through the pages of this book. I have prayed that many burdens will be lifted - including those existing for a long time.

Please be unhurried as you dwell carefully on each page. We can feel that we are coming to the true source of peace in this uncertain world.

May the Lord Jesus (God the Father with us) bless every moment that you spend in His word.

John A. Woolley

Commendations for
Many Mansions

Many people have been and are still being greatly helped by Fr. John Woolley's spiritual books, which have been translated into many other languages. This latest book *Many Mansions* is certainly my favourite of his writings. It stresses the heavenly perspective of our Christian faith which I think is partly neglected.

Father Woolley reminds us in more than one place that: *In My hour of glory, My chosen ones will constantly be engaged upon my mission of love for the children of earth... In My Kingdom you will have the satisfaction of bringing to others the unique help which you yourself received on earth.*

This is not only for the very great saints like St. Therese of Lisieux and Padre Pio, who wrote about it, but by the grace of God for everyone who has our Lord as their hope.

We should, God willing, be looking forward to exercising a ministry of intercession from 'above'. Alleluia!

Dom Benedict Heron OSB
Cockfosters

Like other books of Fr. John Woolley, this latest, *Many Mansions*, is a beautiful and encouraging book, and a real gift of grace.

Fr. Michael Clothier OSB
Downside.

INTRODUCTION

Many Mansions is a sequel to the much-loved devotional books *I Am With You* and *My Burden is Light*.

Like the previous books, *Many Mansions* contains 'heart whispers' received in prayer-time by Fr. John from the risen Lord Jesus Christ.

So many have found a warm sense of God's nearness, and a definite life-changing quality in our Lord's words. Despair has so often given way to hope, and anxiety to tranquillity.

In *Many Mansions*, our Lord gives us

many glimpses of the realm of light which we all long for. Also, he shows us ways of preparing for that future existence while we are still upon the earth.

My child, heaven is the place where you will finally find complete rest for your soul...

Heaven is a *guarded* place, where I have the great joy of seeing My children kept from all false beckonings, and from every kind of danger.

It is here that My children whom I have saved for Myself, share in what they and Myself have been anticipating.

My child, do not be anxious about the hour at which you may eventually leave your earthly existence - simply look forward to the perfect understanding which awaits you.

...to be with the Lord for ever
(1 Thessalonians 4: 7)

1

*F*or My children who have come through an earthly life, with all its trials, the vital characteristic of heaven will be its unchanging *welcome.*

The welcome of heaven is part of the Good News which I came to the earth to bring:

   ... Good News for the fearful;
   ... Good News for those who feel
                         ashamed;
   ... Good News for the despairing;

My children who believe in the message of My Gospel, will now find themselves eager to surrender to the tenderness of heaven's welcome.

**There is no condemnation
for those in Christ Jesus**
(Romans 8: 1)

*A*s you contemplate the vast scale of My universe, you naturally ponder how I can be so attuned to your individual need.

Yes, this is life's great miracle... a creator God who can be lovingly concerned about one of His children.

That concern was shown unmistakably when I forsook all the manifestations of glory, and came to your world in poverty of spirit.

I came to save the lost, and to raise the downtrodden, lifting them that they might one day enter My home of glory.

My child, that is *your* hope...

**Even the hairs of your head
are all counted**
(Luke 12: 7)

My child, never forget the great recompense of heaven.

I know everything that a child of Mine has suffered upon earth. There need be no bitterness at the apparent unfairness of life's trials, because the heavenly recompense will be exactly what will heal the wounds of that child's spirit.

Think only of the joy which one day awaits you, when all the suffering of earth will be forgotten in the midst of your new-found blessings.

A recompense which will be over-flowing!

Those who sow in tears will reap in joy
(Psalm 126: 5)

My child, you may feel that you have faltered badly in pursuing your heavenly inheritance.

But I want you to know that, in My sight, as you endeavour so hard to trust Me, you are still securely on My road because of the *constant covering of My mercy.*

Heaven, is not a prize which is either gained or lost according to man's ordinances; it is not gained or lost by your exposure to life's seeming chances.

When you first invited Me to share your life, you inherited a hope which simply could not be changed!

In heaven is kept a treasure which will not fail you
(Luke 12: 33)

5

*I*t is no vain hope that loved ones whom you have lost on earth are now in the heavenly realm.

Bonds of love formed upon earth, and based upon My care, are made strong to be of eternal duration.

You are always safe to thank Me for My care of those whom you have loved but, for the moment, see no longer.

In My Kingdom there will be great joy among My saved children as they share with loved ones, precious memories, and instances of My rescue from dark places.

**The righteous will
shine like the sun**
(Matthew 13: 43)

*T*he events of life on earth take place within a heavenly framework, which cannot be superficially recognised because it is of a different substance.

You can, however, touch the heavenly whenever you reach out to the Saviour who came expressly to bring heaven within reach of earth.

The pain existing in the created world would be unbearable for so many, if it were not for the eternal consolation which I bring from heaven.

My dear child, that consolation is always there for you.

He heals the broken-hearted
(Psalm 147: 3)

*T*he pathway to heaven...

My child, learn to recognise those blessings of life which create that pathway

If, from the start, your resolve is to come into My near presence one day, you will find so many helps along that way...

　　...the kindnesses of friends
　　...the many seemingly-small
　　　　things which cause you to say a
　　　　heartfelt 'thank you' each day

Not only these, but those moments of looking up to Me in times of suffering... these, too, are part of the pathway, in which a child's inheritance is consolidated.

**Resting on the hope
of eternal life**
(Titus 1: 2)

*A*lways let the knowledge that you have Me with you outweigh everything else!

Even in the worst possible circumstances, whether of sickness, of loss, of failed hopes, My presence will be sufficient for you.

In the thought of Me, you can go on courageously, even though you have no awareness of courage in yourself.

My child, there are times when you realise that I am all that you have. At such times you are simply experiencing what countless children of Mine have experienced. They have then gone on to victory!

I am with you always
(Matthew 28: 20)

Man's greatest fear is not of suffering, or of loss of those greatly loved, or even of death itself.

The greatest fear, all through the ages has been that of *nothingness*... the dread that all the dreams and expectations of life in the material world have been in vain.

My child, if all had been vain hope, I would not have given those sure promises to My disciples when I was on earth. Promises which I convey to your spirit, still, in the present day.

All I ask of you is that you let your thoughts dwell upon Myself, and that you hold fast to My promises in order to dispel the fear of nothingness.

**The Lord is faithful
to all His promises**
(Psalm 145: 13)

*M*y child, there are so many occasions in a single day when I reach out to save you... occasions mostly unnoticed!

It will do so much for your faith as you teach yourself to notice those things which only I could have brought about.

My interventions in the 'small things' as well as in larger matters, are simply acts of anticipation on behalf of a loved one... so often without a need being expressed by that child.

As you recognise My acts of provision you will say, with child-like gratitude, 'That was You; thank You, Lord.'

Before they call, I will answer
(Isaiah 65: 24)

My child, try to see that it is for your good that you cannot always be taken out of the world, with all its pain.

As you frequently struggle with the trials and disappointments of earth, remember the glance to My love, always helping you to endure just a little longer.

Thinking of Me, you are allowing some of the light of heaven to be shed upon your way. You are then *led*, however confused or weak you may feel.

One day you will realise why I did not take you out of the world before I had become precious to you!

I will be with you when you go through deep waters
(Isaiah 43: 2)

*M*y child, think often about why I came to earth. Listen only to the voice of truth which tells you that *I came to save.* Yes, I warned about the dangers of treating eternal life lightly, and to teach My children that heaven would demand perfection... *But I came to save!*

I have always longed for the very slightest softening of the heart where once there had been indifference or rebellion. I constantly see a child's future as heaven when I could woo that child's heart.

My saving work is patient work, as you have found in your own life. Many obstacles are put in the way by evil, but My love never tires. I always see My realm as incomplete where there is someone who needs to know My love.

**God our Saviour wants
all to be saved**
(1 Timothy 2: 4)

$\mathcal{M}$y child, always pursue love!

Be sure to make time for those on earth whom you have found to reflect My love in some way; seek their company, even when life has much else to pre-occupy you.

Judge My children *only* by the love they show, never by what they are able to do for you. Yes, value their love for its own sake.

Welcome love in whatever form it comes - often from surprising sources; it carries My healing, and draws our hearts closer.

I am glorified in them
(John 17:10)

*A*s I strengthen you - and *only* as I strengthen you - you are made able to firmly refuse what is not of Me.

Firstly, the refusal to let anything trouble your spirit! This you do by looking into My light and thanking Me that the matter which troubled you is in My hands... often repeated!

Secondly, *refusing to let life be spoiled,* as I help you to meet the daily imperfections and disappointments courageously.

My child, are you learning to 'hide' in Me, so that what is not of Me is unable to intrude?

Do not let your heart be troubled
(John 14:1)

*N*owhere can you find as complete a turning from sorrow into joy as in My earthly victory.

Before My triumph at the first Easter, there was only despair, heart-brokenness, unbelief, and a sense that the forces of love and of goodness had failed after all.

My child, the joy of Easter (at first experienced by only a few), was ordained to remain as a *permanent* factor of life on earth and, afterwards, of heaven.

For My children even merely to contemplate My saving victory brings a quiet joy.

...things too wonderful for me...
(Psalm 131: 1)

My child, you realise that you are indeed My possession... but I want you to reflect more frequently on My being *your* possession.

It will always be a source of blessing to you when you thank Me that *I belong to you!* You could possess no higher gift.

Yes, My child, I delight in being your permanent possession... always concerned to bring about the highest and very best for you.

All that I ask is that you *value* what is yours. In a life which is barren or disappointing, the gift of Myself can be even more precious.

A pearl of great price
(Matthew 13: 45)

Y ou realise, increasingly, that there is only one place in which to put your hopes, to avoid bitter disappointment.

Disappointment can easily come when you are   guided only by worldly standards in what you strive to bring about.

My child, as far as you can, I want you to *simplify* your life: giving even more time to communion with Me and surrendering all that is on your heart. To show such restraint will not always be easy, but the day-by-day instances of trust rewarded will convince you about the life of simplicity!

Without Me, you can do nothing
(John 15: 5)

*D*o not be deterred by the thought of sheer numbers when contemplating heaven. I know the need of each individual soul who comes to Me from the very unique learning-ground of earth.

Because I control the whole of creation there is perfect knowledge and perfect provision within the Godhead.

What I seek among My children in your present world is that the *requirements* of love should be learned.

If love has not been learned, then My realm would seem to be an alien sphere. My child make up your mind that love for Me and for your fellow-children is your aim.

Love one another...
(John 13: 34)

My child, you will often have felt the wistfulness of desperately wanting the Good News to be true after all.

I, too, have a longing...   a longing for that meeting one day with a child of Mine. I anticipate joyfully the meeting with a child of earth, who is now free from pain, just as I anticipated, joyfully, the meeting with Mary on the Resurrection morning.

As you experience the delights of heaven, I know that you will have a dominant desire for many of My children to share those delights.

**John said to Peter,
'It is the Lord!'**
(John 21: 7)

*A*s you have discovered, blessings can be hidden in the hardships of life. The more obvious blessings are a courage which was previously absent, and a sensitivity to need in others.

But although you may not realise it immediately, My child, there is one over-riding purpose in the suffering which I allow.

That purpose is to unite us!

My good influence is upon your life in order to draw us together. This will reach its consummation in heaven.

That they may be one
(John 17: 11)

*T*he only sounds heard in heaven are those sounds of love which build up your spirit!

The peace which prevails is a peace which accompanies a constant and ordered activity of love.

The peace of My Kingdom blends perfectly with the praise of My children who have come through great trials on earth; they now rest, with deep gratitude, at finally coming home.

My child, My whispers into your heart when on earth have been sounds of heaven!

Peace, be still
(Mark 4: 39)

My child, the whole basis of
our relationship is your utter
dependence. I am always close by
in order to quieten your spirit, and
to give you the sense of being cared
for.

It is at those moments of feeling lost
or afraid that the mere thought that
I have all in My hands will give You
steadiness.

My child, has your heart been given
wholly to Me? Remember how
much I depend on you to minister
to My own heart.

Thus, a *mutual* dependency.

I have called you friends
(John 15: 15)

*I*n a fallen world, there is so much that you could give to Me. Against the background of earth's sin and deception, I find great comfort in every moment which you set aside for Me. I treasure all your child-like trusting and expressions of desire not to fail Me.

My child, I have said that there are few who find the road to life. Those who find it may not be 'achievers' in the worldly sense; rather they are the welcoming hearts where I can live; welcoming hearts in a world which largely rejects My love.

We will make our home in him
(John 14: 23)

All the regrets, all the painful memories bound up with life on earth, will be thankfully laid down on coming into My realm.

At that time all that you will carry is a 'burden of the heart' to be My servant. I will respond to that desire by giving to you, as your very special mission, My lost ones on earth.

One day you will learn more of the angelic ministry, in which My messengers go out from Me in endless ways of provision and rescue for My children.

Let your light shine
(Matthew 5: 16)

*M*y child, never under-estimate
how powerful is the sounding of
My Name in *any* surroundings,
and at any time.

Even whispered, the power is the
same, even though you may have to
summon up all your strength to
utter My Name.

My Name used when, perhaps, all
your heart for living has been lost,
when you are conscious only of
weakness.

My child your frequent use of My
Name...

> bringing courage...
> bringing healing of the spirit...
> uniting us more closely!

**There is no other name under heaven
by which you can be saved.**
(Acts 4: 12)

*A*t the gate of heaven you will be rewarded by seeing the parting of the clouds!

What will be revealed will be the brightness of My Person, bringing healing of all earth's hurt memories.

All that will remain, in memory, will be the *precious* times, times when I came to you...

in unspoiled beauty;
in true affection from human
sources;
to strengthen, when you were
utterly weak;
to convey the *divine affection*,
helping you to feel secure once
again.

Your heart will find happiness
(John 16: 22)

*T*here will always be an attempt by the forces opposed to Me to take you from the path which I have planned for you.

You are saved from this activity of evil by ensuring one vital thing *every day*... that I have the gift of your heart.

This giving of your heart to Me tells Me that your desire is to be with Me one day in that place of unfading light.

The heart given unreservedly to Me enables Me to *already see you* in that place where I am!

**Whoever endures to the
end will be saved**
(Matthew 24: 13)

When you arrive at My home of blessedness, you will not only be able to see Me in surroundings of glory but, looking back, will see Me in the midst of the earth I love!

This is because I am always where there is pain and much suffering in order to transform these things.

So many of My children, experiencing life's pain, nevertheless glimpse the glory which awaits. Perhaps only a glimpse, when life is almost unbearable.

My child, can you see My purpose of pain shared with Me as a preparation for the entry into that glory?

...out of great tribulation
(Revelation 7: 14)

*N*owhere in the whole of existence are you able to recover so rapidly from the misfortunes of life as you can by calling upon Me.

In your very deepest hurts, the world is so often powerless to enter the wounded places and bring peace. All that is left for you is to fly to Me! There, in My arms, wanting only to rest in My love, you can let Me restore your wounded spirit.

If only the world realised how much is achieved by the *sureness* of My working.

I am the Lord who heals you
(Exodus 15: 26)

*I*t was in the setting of a world of wickedness and despair, a world of cruelty and injustice, that I spoke of the hope of heaven.

The *only* element of hope for My children, who have experienced the world's suffering, is a future in My presence.

The frequent times of darkness in the present existence bring to the human heart a very natural longing...

My child, believe with all your being that that longing *will be met*; it is based upon My promises and, therefore, is to be trusted.

God will wipe away every tear
(Revelation 7: 17)

One day it will be your great
pleasure to enter the unlimited
sphere of the Father's heavenly
home which I (as the expression of
the Father), promised to prepare
for you.

Here you will enjoy the fullest
consciousness of My fatherly
protection.

Here, there will be delights which
are unspoiled, as a reward for
simple trust and faithful allegiance
while in My world.

My child, in your heavenly home
you will be aware that *even more*
blessing awaits you!

I go to prepare a place for you
(John 14: 2)

*E*very step taken towards Myself when you pray is a step into heaven.

Yes, even the most faltering step!

You then take back into the complexities of your world, the atmosphere of My Kingdom.

Yes, how *vital* are your prayers...

My child, the mere thought of the heavenly places must give you courage and keep your hope alive when all seems lost.

Remember that the vastness of the heavenly realm is only equalled by the vastness of My love.

The Lord will save:
He will delight in you
(Isaiah 62: 4)

*A*s you reverence Me and bring Me into every conceivable earthly circumstance you will be no stranger to heaven, when you arrive there one day.

The *music* of heaven, reflecting all that has been sweet and peace-giving on earth.

The *brightness* of heaven reflecting those earthly occasions of joyful reconciliation after the darkness of discord.

No stranger to heaven!... a hand of love and warmth to clasp your own as you enter.

**Well done,
good and faithful servant**
(Matthew 25: 21)

My child, the *angelic vocation*...

In My home of glory, My chosen ones will constantly be engaged upon My mission of love for the children of earth.

The angelic messengers will always be sent at the precise moment of need, bringing spontaneous expressions of gratitude at a danger averted or a pressing need supplied. The angelic source of the help received will not always be recognised!

In My kingdom you will have the satisfaction of bringing to others the unique help which you yourself received on earth.

He will feed His flock like a shepherd
(Isaiah 40: 11)

My child, there are so many burdens to be shed before arrival at heaven's gate.

The most desirable state for a child who has left behind the burdens of earth, is that of *self-forgetfulness*. The focus of that child will now be upon Myself and upon the many souls needing to hear the healing words of My gospel.

The light of My love will shine for those hurting souls to show them that their days of suffering have ended.

Yours can be the privilege of helping to bring this about!

I will heal all that they have done and love them freely
(Hosea 14: 4)

*M*y child, as I look upon you at *any* stage of your life, I still see the little child whom I ushered into the world.

The little child may have been lost to view by life's harmful experiences, but My fatherly vision of you never changes.

Desire *only* what is for your eternal good to remain from what has been in your life and let Me remove all else.

After heaven is reached, I look for a child whose spirit has been purified by a willingness to completely surrender to Me.

**A mother may forget her child,
but I will not forget you**
(Isaiah 49: 15)

My Kingdom is extended whenever a child whose heart has been given to Me reaches, in some way, another earthly child.

My child, is that the set of your own heart... the advance of My Kingdom? Be assured that I will complete, in My sure way, all that you feel led to do for Me.

I use those things which are natural to you... the giving of an encouraging word, a warm 'thank you', a simple act of support, a mere smile, even.

Yes, in all these things, heaven breaks through!

You are the world's salt
(Matthew 5: 13)

*T*he only real stability in your present world is found when, in your life, there is one hope, one fixed point.

If I am that one fixed point, you will not be led astray by the false hopes which are presented to you by the world.

You will then find that you can always return to Me when conscious of failure.

The *blessing* of being back in My arms!

You are blest, My child, that you fixed *your* hope on Him who is unchanging.

Lord, to whom else can we go?
(John 6: 68)

My child, do you have the longing that I will be there to greet you at the end of your earthly life? If you have this longing, it will always tell you, beyond argument, that you are My chosen!

In the midst of earthly struggles, thank Me, in sheer trust, that I will go ahead of you and reveal to you that your hope has not been in vain.

What will be revealed will be a beauty excelling all that you have experienced... a beauty which is simply a manifestation of My love.

My child, *trust* that longing...

Loved with everlasting love...
(Jeremiah 13: 3)

My child, why do you deprive
yourself?

You are never deprived of the
important things if you resolutely
make much time for Me each day.

From these moments of waiting
upon Me, the gifts of an eternal
character are yours... true peace,
enlightenment, deepening of faith,
and a greater appreciation of
Myself.

In those moments, I am at work
on many aspects of your life
from which you may have been
distracted. But, of course, they
were in *My* mind!

This is the measure of My concern...
furthering your interests when you
yourself may be distracted!

Only one thing is vital
(Luke 10: 42)

On your earthly journey you have so often been in the heavenly realm without fully realising it.

At the end of that journey, those things which are not of Me, and which have troubled you, will exist no longer, and you will be able to experience heaven to your great pleasure.

I know, My child, that you would gladly escape many of the hard places of your existence and simply 'come home' to where I dwell. Be assured that I will make the hard places a sure preparation for you. In those hard places you will find the grace to wait patiently, in the knowledge that all will be 'made right'.

**I have chosen you
out of the world**
(John 15: 19)

*W*hen many things crowd into your mind at one time, including what seem to be pressing duties, I want you, very deliberately, to *pause*, and bring each individual matter to Me.

This brief pause in your life equips you the more perfectly for what you have to attend to.

As you wait upon Me, certain matters will 'light up' for you as the most urgent or important.

As you deal, unhurriedly, with what I show you in this way, I will always give you time with which to attend to other matters!

The Lord gives wisdom
(Proverbs 2: 6)

*M*y child, even if your natural temperament is to be fearful, do you believe that I can make you able to fear nothing?

Remember that fear is evil's weapon upon earth and this is why your choice of Myself as your Friend is such a vital step.

As you learn to rest securely in My arms and, in spite of all, look forward to a future with Me, even fears of long standing will lose their hold upon you.

The future for you, My child, is the realm where fear is unknown.

Perfect love casts out fear
(1 John 4: 18)

*M*y child, at the end of your earthly journey, your principal hope should be that of *coming to live with Me.*

It is wisdom, therefore, to learn true appreciation of Myself while on earth.

> Learning to let My love comfort you.
> Learning to allow My working in matters beyond your control.
> Learning to say a quiet and heart-felt thanks for the small things.
> Noticing My hand in life's co-incidences and the instances of provision in your favour.

Gratitude is a *sure* preparation for heaven!

**Trust in the Lord
with all your heart**
(Proverbs 3: 5)

$\mathcal{M}$y child, pain is not unknown in love's realm...

Pain is a true ingredient of heavenly joy because pain is part of the 'suffering overcome' which you share with Me.

The fullness of joy which I promised contains the elements of victory; a victory which would not be there in the absence of suffering.

On earth, you have come to see that suffering and a sense of My love can exist together. This is a prelude to the unalloyed joy which awaits My chosen ones in My Kingdom.

**Whoever overcomes
will inherit all things**
(Revelation 21: 7)

*M*y child, can you look up from the greyness of those dark valleys? With your mind's eye can you see the blue of heaven instead of the greyness around you? If you can, even for a few moments, you will find courage.

Thanksgiving to Me in the midst of pain, brings you into the company of My chosen children through the ages who were able to see victories brought out of many hardships.

Your 'thank You, Lord' may be barely a whisper (often tearful) but it has made a little more sure your eternal hope.

**Give thanks to the Lord
for He is good**
(Psalm 107: 1)

$\mathcal{M}$y child, *I go before you always.*

I go before you, with My peace-making influence, into those occasions about which you feel misgivings, even fear.

Can you see how, so many times, a situation which caused you dread was averted?

Can you see how circumstances reached a conclusion which otherwise they would not have done?

I went before you, just as I go before you into My Kingdom!

**My sheep hear My voice,
and they follow Me**
(John 10: 27)

You will be more and more filled with wonder at My provision for you.

You will know for certain that I have been at work for you when you see aspects of your existence 'coming together' in a wonderful way, without any effort on your part. This will always be at precisely the right time for you.

The uniqueness of My road of life is that a child whose heart has been given to Me is *carried* along that road.

True obedience is always effortless, *if I partner you...*

Rest in the Lord
(Psalm 37: 7)

*S*ee My hand reaching out to you, guiding you through a spoiled and sad creation to the realm of truth, where you will *know* what has long been planned for you.

My child, is simply to be with Me your earnest wish? If this is so, nothing in your present world will ever be allowed to spoil your spiritual progress.

All evil's attempts to spoil your progress will be brought to nothing.

I lead you to a destination with your eternal bliss in mind!

**He leads me
beside still waters**
(Psalm 23: 2)

My child, cultivate the highest ambition... to be love's messenger!

If I use you in this way, your identity may be unknown, but your deeds will be recognised as of Me.

Those deeds will involve countless instances of rescue, and of provision in great need.

Those on earth who see My hand in the various instances of help, and thank Me, are greatly blessed. They too, are prepared for the angelic realm.

Yes, My child, be even more alert to recognise My working...

**I came to search for the lost
and to save them**
(Luke 19: 10)

*A*t the end of your earthly life the sheer brightness of My presence will help you to leave behind everything tainted by life in the world.

Remember that heaven is essentially a reward for *trusting*, even in a life with many imperfections.

In the brightness which you find as you enter heaven, you will have no other desire than to know Me as I have known you.

Yes, My child, *I Myself* am heaven's reward! That is why your trust is rewarded by My presence ministering to you *long before heaven is reached.*

**The crown of glory
that will never fade**
(1 Peter 5: 4)

*M*y committed children upon earth have learned, as an important principle, the conscious receiving of love, and the reaching-out in love.

The reaching-out in love is a natural and grateful response to having experienced, and fed upon, the divine love. In My Kingdom, the principle learned will be seen to perfection.

My child, in heaven's service, all your unfulfilled longings for love will be met, and by your own presence, others will receive from you something of the love of the world's Saviour

I am sending you out...
(Matthew 10: 16)

*W*hen earth is left behind, all evil's deceptions, assailing the mind, will be consigned to the past.

When deception is listened to, so much love is prevented from being received; a child may suffer a complete lack of self-worth and a constant sense of insecurity. When deception is listened to, a child is prevented from reaching that of which he or she is capable.

In heaven you will no longer be pulled down by deception, but free to enjoy My love as never before, and free to express Me with a new-found confidence.

The truth will set you free
(John 8: 32)

*M*y child, the longer our acquaintance lasts, the stronger will be your conviction that in desperate need only I will suffice.

At times of being very afraid, only I am able to reach into your heart and speak the peace of My love.

My child, when you cry out to Me because you are overwhelmed, it always touches My heart.

If you have, as a habit, reached out to My love, it will become increasingly natural for you to do so *immediately* when need is desperate.

Given power from heaven
(Luke 24: 49)

My child, consider these examples of what can be experienced on earth:

> The sun breaking through after
>   rain;
> The return to health after illness;
> Goodwill in someone previously
>   hostile;
> The return of faith after a long
>   period of unbelief.

These aspects of an imperfect world can point to the ultimate heavenly experience.

Where life has meant great struggle for you (often almost unbearable) the great *contrast*, on finding the realm of light, will be all the more precious to you.

To see My glory
(John 17: 24)

When you pray for someone to find My love (which is the highest you could ask), then you are sharing in My wish for the ultimate destiny of every one of My children.

You will be aware that the knowledge of My love can exist simultaneously with the various forms of suffering; My love giving the will to endure. The peace which you feel when you even contemplate My love is just one of the compensations of human suffering.

My child, I know you would wish My children to have an inner certainty of My love as they inhabit eternity!

**I will create a pathway
in the wilderness**
(Isaiah 43: 19)

You will never know the multitude of things from which I have saved you!

My child, try to see as 'right', in some way, all that I *do* allow in your life, including those things hard to understand. Those things carry a concealed blessing which one day you will see.

It gives Me great consolation when you say a quiet 'thank you' for what is, for the moment, painful.

All that I ask of a child tenderly cared for in a creation where so much is threatening, is your grateful heart.

**I will care for you
to the end**
(Isaiah 46: 4)

*T*he darker episodes of life are, nevertheless, all part of the *heavenly* experience...

Can you see that pain is not unknown in heaven's learning-ground?

Yes, release from all pain is My purpose for you, but experiences of life's pain can be part of your being made ready. As you willingly share, with Me, such pain, you are being made ready for heaven's unique ministry, when your earthly life is over.

My child, are you willing for that ministry to be yours one day?

**Where I am, there
will My servant be**
(John 12: 26)

*T*he various forms of 'loss' upon earth can be heartbreaking, and often you will find it almost impossible to give thanks for what has occurred.

My child, I want you (even as a cold and dutiful thing, perhaps in the midst of tears), to express your thanks to Me in order that under My hand, the earthly loss can become, for you, a heavenly gain.

When any of life's terribly sad occurrences are surrendered to My enfolding love, they contain the hope of future good. This is the hope to which you trustingly cling in the midst of your shock and, so often, through your tears.

All things work together for good for those who love the Lord
(Romans 8: 28)

$\mathcal{M}$y child, just as I observe all that happens in My creation, I watch over the *details* of your life. Nothing is too unimportant to be referred to Me.

Major moves in your life can result from seemingly small steps taken *with Me in mind*. I mould everything into what will be to your advantage.

It is not fearful caution to carefully share every step with Me, wanting to avoid what could be disastrous.

It is not fear; it is wisdom!

I will go with you and prosper all that you do
(Exodus 33:14)

My child, the only wise preparation for a future home in heaven is to *value what is of Me* in your earthly existence:

> To value all instances of great and sacrificial kindness, knowing they are of Me;

> To value earthly scenes of great beauty;

> To value all that uplifts the spirit;

> To value all instances of human *faithfulness*;

Although these things may only be pale reflections of what you will find in heaven, thank Me whenever you encounter them.

...the hem of his garment
(Luke 8: 44)

My child, learn the nature of My working...

Firstly, it is to bring about what I see is best for the surrendered heart;

Secondly, it is to take the circumstances given to Me, and to make them serve a good purpose;

Thirdly, it is to work upon the human situation of a child of Mine so that all may be *made right*.

You can therefore thankfully give yourself, wholeheartedly, into My love, knowing these things.

The peace of placing everything out of your fallible hands into Mine!

You will find rest for your soul
(Matthew 11: 29)

$\mathcal{M}$y peace, stealing upon you when all is turbulent... something which only My children who trust Me can experience.

The sense of peace is telling you that beyond the storm all *must* be well; it is the peace which comes to a child who simply clings desperately to Me when life is overwhelming.

My child, circumstances so often seem to say that you ought not to be experiencing calm! But remember that My peace is a *unique* gift, guarding your heart.

He is our peace
(Ephesians 2: 14)

γou may not be conscious of it,
but there is an influence upon all
your relationships and encounters.
It is the influence of heaven! Under
the divine influence, every word
(even said casually or thoughtlessly)
has significance.

Whenever there is an atmosphere of
love and understanding, you can be
sure that the influence of heaven has
prevailed.

When a hitherto-strained, even
acrimonious, relationship gives way
to one of reasonableness and
affection, heaven's whole-making
influence has been at work.

He ran out and embraced him
(Luke 15: 20)

My child, the desire...

In a fallen world, where your weakness will often cause you to stray (even momentarily), keep that steady desire to be *with Me* always and to learn of Me.

I *always* respond to the heart which reaches out to Me... a reaching-out which builds up your own consciousness that I can never fail you.

You will always need to be vigilant in view of evil's wish to take you away from Me... vigilant, above all, in nurturing that steady desire!

Set your mind on things above
(Colossians 3: 2)

*O*n earth, there are those of great worth whose friendship you have treasured... perhaps only one or two.

My child, understand that such friendships are never eclipsed by My own love for you. You will find that My love blends with all that is of love and goodness in the world, however humble the human vessels.

Nothing which, even in the most imperfect way, reflects Myself, can ever be lost to your experience.

Everything of *love* in heaven or upon earth, is of *eternal* worth.

We love, because He first loved us
(1 John 4: 19)

$\mathcal{Y}$ ou realise that the attempts of evil to turn hearts away from Me will finally fail.

I only permit evil's activity where it will eventually increase dependence on Myself. Countless hearts, crying out to Me from the darkness caused by evil, have come to trust Me.

One of the great blessings of reaching heaven will be to know that the powers of darkness will be unable to trouble your spirit any longer!

My victory has always rejoiced the hosts of heaven...

**I saw Satan fall
like lightning**
(Luke 10: 18)

*S*o many things on earth offer temporary support... support when worn down by life's chances, support when criticised or misunderstood, support when you feel utterly overwhelmed...

What you receive when you reach the heavenly places is completely unlike the fragile refuges of support of the material world.

Within the *heavenly* refuge, your security will be such that you are able to turn, in love, to the needs of many of My other children.

My child, look forward to this!

**The Name of the Lord
is a strong tower**
(Proverbs 18: 10)

$\mathcal{M}$y child, why were you chosen?

Why have I drawn you to know Me?

My choice of you goes back to the very earliest days of your existence.

At that time, I knew that you would respond to My love, even if all that you are now aware of is your lack of faithfulness.

My choosing of you creates a bond between us which simply cannot be broken... a bond made safe in your eventual home with Me.

**Drawn to Myself
with loving-kindness**
(Jeremiah 31: 3)

*B*ecause My love cannot be earned, and is My gift, I ensure that the awareness of My love is never lost, even if your trust is a trembling and imperfect one.

Be content to think *only* of My love whenever there is opportunity, and remember that My love's activity on your behalf is based on just one thing... your *need*.

My child, My love is best understood in its *automatic response* to your need, which is always before Me!

Never doubt that I wish, profoundly, to see your need met, and that this is *not* dependant on merit.

The greatest of these is love
(1 Corinthians 13: 13)

*M*y child, never forget that your prayers for others can have *eternal* significance.

Is your earnest prayer that someone should know My love? The knowledge of My love, if acted upon, will be there to carry that child through the gate of heaven.

You see what a great privilege it is to lead another child into knowing My love! Often it will be your prayer alone - after which, you can safely leave a person's heart to Me.

The extent of love's influence... seen in your own experience of My love *bearing fruit* on behalf of another child.

**Whatever you ask in prayer, believe
that it is granted, and it will be so**
(Mark 11: 24)

My child, ensure that a grateful heart does not waver throughout life. Ponder some of the many things which touch My heart...

My heart is gladdened by each simple act of kindness which lifts the spirit of another of My children and My heart is *always* deeply touched when, in painful circumstances, you tell Me of your belief that *all is not lost.*

When you come, one day, to the heavenly home of My children, you will know that your thankfulness has been justified.

In My Kingdom there is, already, a multitude of thankful souls!

In everything give thanks...
(1 Thessalonians 5: 18)

*A*s you learn to recognise My working in your life, you will be moved to say a word of thanksgiving for so many things:

a totally unexpected kindness;

a danger averted

a fleeting word from a friend which helped or encouraged.

When such things happen, you will be increasingly able to see My hand in what came to you.

My child, recognising *My* touch in your day-to-day circumstances will help to allay so much fear of the future.

The birds, who do not sow, are fed by your heavenly Father
(Matthew 6: 26)

My child as you ponder the harder aspects of life on earth, be assured that in My Kingdom, the opposing qualities have been prepared for you:

for sadness, the quality of joy;
for fear, tranquillity
for cruelty, tenderness
for resentment, an overwhelming forgiveness
for timidity, a courage, inspired by me.
for deception, truth in all its beauty;
for doubt and misgivings, a trust which cannot be shaken;
for despair, an unswerving hope

The brightness of My love will shine through all.

I am making everything new
(Revelation 21: 5)

My care for you as an *individual* will be unchanged when you dwell among the hosts of heaven.

By no means will you feel 'lost'!

The unique communion between us will be free of all distractions, as our relationship (which was begun on earth) is further fed.

You will become even more certain that the only thing which matters is My love for you.

Your vision of existence will be enlarged, and you will be able to pray with more love in your heart for My suffering and lost ones.

**The Lord God will be
your everlasting light**
(Isaiah 60: 19)

*W*hen, on earth, you make the choice to follow Me, you are really choosing freedom for living!

One of the great gifts involved in the freedom of following Me is that of not being under coercion to choose wrongly. So many who do not know Me are constantly making unwise choices because they do not recognise the subtle pressures upon them.

You know, of course, that freedom was won for you by My conquest of evil forces.

My child, you truly are free if you simply value the *friendship* which is yours.

Where the Spirit of the Lord is, there is freedom
(2 Corinthians 3: 17)

My child, when you find yourself in one of the world's many threatening situations, there may come, very quietly, a feeling of hope which seems quite illogical.

Often you simply cannot see how the situation will be resolved and yet somehow, you know that hope exists because you have My presence with you.

In the life of a child who trusts Me, a feeling of *quiet expectation* will often be experienced, in spite of difficult circumstances. In My heavenly Kingdom you will know the true fulfilment of such expectation.

The peace which transcends all understanding
(Philippians 4: 7)

My child, I want you to develop the gift of *rapid recognition*. Especially, you need to recognise states which have become habitual and harmful in your thinking.

Recognise dread of the future for what it is, and remember, instead, My promise to care for you to the end. Let that same promise help you to avoid all paralysing self-concern.

Be vigilant in not allowing anything other than hope, knowing My utter faithfulness!

If your sense of My love is not allowed to die, hope will always be nearby to carry you through.

**Little flock
you must not be afraid**
(Luke 12: 32)

*T*he best preparation for the longed-for moment of entry into heaven is to shed all that is of self (in all its subtlety) and all that is not of truth.

For your encouragement, I want you to know that immersing yourself in Me (always returning to Me in your thoughts, after distraction), will gradually overcome self.

Earth has so many opportunities for making ready your spirit, with eternity in mind.

My child, even to look at Me, trustingly, is a quiet victory over 'self'!

Blessed are those with pure hearts; they will see God
(Matthew 5: 8)

*M*y child, you can indeed anticipate the sight of your risen and glorified Lord when you reach the heavenly places... the vision of the majesty of the Godhead dwelling in Me.

Until that day, let the desire for all that is of Me, burn steadily.

As you cling to that desire at all costs, you will find that the inroads of evil will never be able to take My in-dwelling presence from you.

To share My resurrection will be the reward for your faithfulness and trust.

**Christ in you,
the hope of glory**
(Colossians 1: 27)

$\mathcal{M}$y child, the *dissolving* power of My light...

The divine light allows no intrusions of the world's darkness if you consciously live in it. Therefore, lose no time in holding up in My light those things which threaten your peace.

All fear, all wrong intentions, the imperfections of others... all to be dissolved in the light of My love!

The light into which you gaze with your heart towards Me is real and lasting. All else is transient and illusory.

Light has come into the world
(John 3: 19)

*T*o see the world around you with clarity, I need to lend you the eye of both love and of truth. This will ensure that your reactions are composed, and that there is neither despair nor a tendency to be judgmental.

As you see more and more with My eye, you will see so many things of earth surrounded by the element of hope. Therefore there can be (with justification) a true looking forward.

Yes, My child, the world's darkness is *moulded* into a realm of future delight, as you trust Me. Again, this is something which I am gratified to do for you.

Leading you into all truth
(John 16: 13)

*T*here are so many ways in which the influence of the *real* world (the heavenly realm) is brought to you upon earth.

Under that influence you are constantly upheld, and I deal with those many things which are outside your direct control.

Under that same influence you are helped to see life's temporary manifestations clearly and to avoid unwise intentions.

The complexities of life make it imperative for a child of Mine to consciously bring *everything* under My influence.

My thoughts are not your thoughts
(Isaiah 15: 8)

*T*he more you surrender to Me
on your earthly journey (giving Me
as much trust as you possibly can)
the more safe and sure will be your
arrival at the realm I have promised.

Always remember that I know the
way! You do not have to create
the way either by striving or by
calculated 'good works'.

Because the road through life, as
you have found, is full of hazards,
always look intently at He who
carries you. Your look will always
bring a sense of My approval!

Led beside water springs...
(Isaiah 49: 10)

*W*hen you make that glad entrance into My heavenly home you will be able to greet those with pure hearts who have endured many years of suffering.

My child, you will then be *part of heaven* and ready to extend your hand to others of My children as they complete their journey.

What once seemed a mere dream will now be there before you... a realm ready to make your own.

In this realm, which is now yours by right, you will be able to *share* My glad task of welcoming!

So that your joy may be complete
(John 15: 20)

*A*lthough I am revealed to you in so many different ways within the fleeting experiences of the material world, I have patiently made you aware of one attribute of Mine which is always there to fly to... Yes, My love!

There will be many delights in the heavenly sphere for My faithful ones, but none will equal the enjoyment of My patient and tender love. The joys of the heavenly places will merely show up My love even more clearly.

My child, the highest calling for you is to be one whom I send to put that love into the hearts of those in earthly darkness.

I will give to drink from the spring of the water of life
(Revelation 21: 6)

My child, does the way I have
provided for you and kept you safe
show you so clearly that you are,
indeed, My chosen? As my chosen,
believe in your heart that you
possess all needed to come through
earth's fluctuations.

Sadly, those who do not trust Me are
at the mercy of so many dangers.
But understand, My child, that even
if one of such children discovers
trust only at a very late stage, I am
pledged to meet that person's need.

Always remember our *unity*... not
only at times of quiet communion
with Myself, but *especially* in the
midst of life's restlessness.

My grace is sufficient for you
(2 Corinthians 12: 9)

$\mathcal{Y}$ou could easily be despondent if you were exposed to the deceptions and intense disappointments of life without a divine Friend to share with you.

My child, an intimation of My love is always there for you; a love which dissolves the hurts and lack of understanding you meet in others.

Whenever you hide in Me and whisper My Name, you find a tranquillity which is quite independent of your circumstances, soothing all hurt, drawing us closer than ever.

The eternal God is your refuge
(Deuteronomy 33: 27)

$\mathcal{M}$y child, I tell you again that your time of great need is the unique opportunity for My love (not adulterated by worldly pre-occupations) to minister to you.

Few of My children upon earth realise the desperate urgency of forming a relationship with Myself which can stand firm in *any* eventuality.

On the heavenward journey, learn to look nowhere but to Me, in order to sense that love.

On that vital journey, the *divine and inseparable Companion* is essential.

**A friend who sticks
closer than a brother**
(Proverbs 18: 24)

*M*y child, the unseen...

All the time, the influence of My Kingdom is transforming the events of your life... even the commonplace ones.

Anything that has been transformed under My influence becomes a *permanent* part of existence, and can be utterly trusted.

Remember to see *every* aspect of your life in the light of My surrounding love... this will help you to observe the very careful walk which I have laid down as the narrow way. Life's aspects *saturated* by My love!

A walk of *safety*...

There is no other Saviour
(Isaiah 43: 11)

Since I left the earth I have been further preparing a place for you, My child, and for other trusting souls. It is a task which gives Me great joy, in anticipation of the entry of My children into the realm of My love.

I do not look, at first, for attainment of virtues (although this is so important); I look, above all, for the heart given to Me, with no holding back.

Yes, a child who is made ready to continue a ministry to the needy, begun on earth.

**By this is My Father glorified,
that you bear much fruit**
(John 15: 8)

My child, the created world is, as you know, the scene of the continuing struggle between the forces of darkness and all that is of Me.

Yes, it is still a dark and fallen world - only partially redeemed. Only the power of love can offer hope.

Never under-estimate the conflict which underlies existence, but let gratitude fill your heart that you have a Friend whose purposes *must* be fulfilled.

Until that day of fulfilment, My light, if sought earnestly, will always pierce the darkness for you and shine on that sure way to heaven!

**Light which the darkness
has never overcome**
(John 1: 5)

When you reach the heavenly realm, there will be a continuation of those most precious times of communion with Me which you began on earth.

I have, still, so much to teach My children about the mysteries of existence. I will speak of My wisdom and patient understanding as springing from My love and of My conquest of evil for you as springing from the same love.

As you wait upon Me, there is always a transforming influence upon your thoughts and intentions to make your life more harmonious with My own.

Learn of Me...
(Matthew 11: 29)

My child, consider what you really wish to achieve as your preparation for being in My near presence.

What is of eternal worth for you to pursue? You will not go seriously astray if your aims are:

　　patiently working to bring My lost ones to Me

　　speaking a word which introduces a sense of My love (perhaps for the first time), where there is despair

　　comforting My own heart by your trust and faithfulness

In it all, remember that I work with you!

The harvest is plenteous...
(Matthew 9: 37)

*M*y child, is your desire the same as My own... a growing *unity* between us?

As you know, the aim of Satanic forces is to divide us, even more than to tempt you to wrong ways.

If you pursue a course which takes you, even temporarily, out of the covering of My love, then you are in danger. I promise to give you a sense of the loss of My presence, that you may turn from any lure away from Me.

Our unity. It is vital that on your earthly journey you will feel thoroughly at ease with your Friend!

Watch and pray
(Matthew 26: 41)

*I*n the heavenly places there is perfect *equality* in every aspect. Earthly attainment will be forgotten, and will not be called for in the new sphere.

You will see all your companions in a new way. Your concern, and that of others in My realm, will be the lost ones of earth, and how I can be made known to them through yourselves.

The satisfaction found in earthly service for Me will now be greatly enhanced.

Yes, My child, a messenger of the divine!

He who began a good work in you will carry it to completion
(Philippians 1: 6)

$\mathcal{M}$y child, it is a deception that My followers must expect to 'feel strong' before serving Me. You do not always reach out to My children in their need from a position of strength.

I have always used 'weak vessels' who have very little else except trust in Me!

Your wish to serve Me will always be accompanied by a *heavenly* 'making-strong' which you yourself may not feel. Your limitations are simply opportunities for Me to demonstrate what I can do, merely in response to your willingness.

You are My servant, and will bring glory to My Name
(Isaiah 49: 3)

*W*hen you 'surprised yourself' by acting out of character in overcoming life's difficulties, it was My presence in you which brought it about. You had been conscious, not of the effort you were making, but of Myself!

Glory is brought to My Name whenever a child of Mine acts against usual inclination and shows great courage or kindness or tranquillity in spite of inward struggles.

Acknowledging your dependency enables Me to strengthen you in the hour of need, in order to surprise both yourself and others.

By your love, people will know that you are My disciples
(John 13: 35)

*A*s you have realised, My child, the road which will take you to heaven is not without its enticements to divert you from your true destiny.

Therefore, make sure that I am very much in your thoughts. I will then constantly step into your life (in ways often unknown to you) to ensure your safety.

For your consolation, I give you the assurance that although you may from time to time, wander into danger, I will never let you be *completely* separated from My love's covering.

**Under the shadow
of the Almighty...**
(Psalm 91: 1)

My child, I know that it is not easy to give thanks when all is darkness. This step of faith can be almost impossible for you.

Let Me help you to glimpse My love through the darkness so that the memory of all that I have been to you will speak quietly to you once again.

You will find courage to thank Me for what lies *beyond* the darkness.

It is a courage (albeit a fragile one) which is slowly becoming part of you...

Inwardly renewed every day...
(2 Corinthians 4: 16)

$\mathcal{B}$efore you bring any matter before Me in prayer, tell Me of your trust, both in My love and in My control of everything in creation.

This brief examination of your trust in our relationship is important because the prayer now becomes one of real faith. On earth, as I have told you, your trust in Me is all that really matters, and is what I look for, above all else.

My child, where I am *really* trusted, the road to heaven will simply open out before you.

**Blessed is He who
trusts in the Lord**
(Proverbs 16: 20)

*M*y child, many more
things than you realise have
love-opportunities in them. Always
give time to such opportunities.

Do not delay an act of love and
kindness in favour of one of life's
more pressing 'self-seeking' matters.

An act of love can often be a simple
and undemanding routine thing on
your part, *made perfect by My blessing
upon it*. You can then rest in the
knowledge that *My* love has been
conveyed.

You created a love-opportunity for
Me!

Risen with healing in His wings
(Malachi 4: 2)

*C*onfronted by others' need you may be conscious, only, at that time, of *your own* weakness and burning sense of need!

Only when heaven is reached can you feel completely liberated in carrying out My mission of love. Until that time you will have to follow the pattern of My saints in history and allow yourself to be a source of strength when feeling weakness.

My child, it is no co-incidence that you feel 'lifted up' (even for a little time, at least), when reaching out to a needy person.

**Strengthened in
every good deed**
(2 Thessalonians 2: 17)

$\mathcal{Y}$ou would very easily become despairing if you forgot, even for a moment or two, My constant working...

And, of course, My working with *you* in mind!

So much of My work is anticipatory (knowing your future) and is unlike your own efforts, which are so often a reaction to events.

My child, how much a chosen child can simply leave with Me, rather than striving. Countless experiences of My faithfulness on the road to heaven!

Cast all your cares upon Him
(Psalm 55: 22)

My interventions in the historical process have a primary purpose... that of removing anything which hinders your progress to the heavenly sphere.

When you really trust Me, you will increasingly recognise what could only have been brought about by Myself.

My child, if I am your hope, you will often experience the miraculous... sometimes spectacular and unmistakable, sometimes very quiet, but still giving you a feeling of awe.

Above all, a grateful child!

The ways of the Lord are sure
(Psalm 19: 9)

*B*efore My victory for My children upon earth, realism about the darker side of life could only lead to despair.

But, My child, you know that after My victory, the same realism can be there but now with an element of *hope*.

The suffering borne by My children on earth will still be in their consciousness on entering My Kingdom... but a consciousness not, now, of pain, but of My love's *sharing*.

Yes, My child, suffering faced and acknowledged. But, because I share, it is transformed into what is truly a heavenly peace.

We know that suffering produces perseverance... and God has poured His love into our hearts.

(Romans 5: 3)

It is the *influence* of My love which carries you gently, but surely, along the heavenward road.

It is My love's influence which makes you strong in carrying out My purposes when you feel anything but strong. Love's silent and unerring influence is at work, *even when your thoughts may not be of Me.*

When I am utterly trusted, the influence of My love will always prove stronger than all other influences.

A spring of water, welling up into eternal life
(John 4: 14)

So many motivations are flawed, even in the realm of 'serving Me' upon earth.

In the heavenly places My children will have in their hearts the extension of My kingdom *out of love for Me.* This will be their one motivation.

My child, tell Me of your wish to see My Kingdom go forward... then look forward to the Kingdom's unmistakable presence throughout the universe.

This is no mere dream!

Your Kingdom come
(Matthew 6: 10)

*U*pon earth, you so often have to hold on desperately to My love in a strange or frightening environment.

My child, be consoled that in My heavenly home , the sole environment is that of love. Here you feel completely 'at home', supported just by the environment.

In My Kingdom, your only desire will be to be part of My mission to those still needing to find Me. You will rejoice when they, too, can feel 'at home' in My love.

**...to share in the inheritance
of the saints**
(Colossians 1: 12)

A gift, as conveyed on earth, is not always a gift in the fullest sense; so often it is an appreciative response to someone's kindness or loyalty.

The one *pure* gift (beyond all price) is that of My Person. I delight to convey Myself to My children out of sheer love.

Never doubt, My child, that despite many failures and feelings of shame, the gift of Myself has been yours from the very moment you sought Me.

I count everything as loss, compared with the all-surpassing knowledge of Jesus Christ my Lord.
(Philippians 3: 8)

My child, you realise that the state of perfection may never be reached in an earthly life but I already see the child who has given his or her life to Me as one day perfected; so take heart! Heaven's delights will be enjoyed to the full in that state of perfection.

Through yourself, as a perfected soul, I will touch many other children.

Remember that true perfection is not the result of striving, but of being soaked in My presence!

Keep yourselves in the love of God
(Jude 21)

You cannot pursue a safe course through life without a Friend to prompt you, constantly.

My children are in the midst of a battle, and the powers of evil never cease in tempting you to leave the place of safety.

If you fix your gaze upon Me, you will know My prompting; you will see life's manifestations for what they really are, and know what can be trusted.

Remember that evil is *made powerless* when you speak My Name.

So then, stand firm...
(2 Thessalonians 2: 15)

*E*ven when you are still in the shock of a difficult circumstance, try to quietly thank Me that I am allowing this (knowing in your heart that I am turning it to good).

This, in itself, will give you the patience you need until you can see what I am bringing about for you.

Those who have given me their allegiance, and know suffering, are among the most privileged of My children. They are able to see how perfectly I make things right out of seemingly-impossible situations.

**The Lord is my helper;
I will not be afraid...**
(Hebrews 13: 6)

*B*ecause the many choices of life on earth are bewildering, there is a natural fear of mistakenly choosing a direction which could prove disastrous for you.

In the midst of these choices and awesome possibilities, you will always find steadiness in the thought of the one direction which is *already planned* for you.

Tell Me of your willingness to follow that direction, in which you will be enfolded, constantly, by the love which was there since you were born.

My child let this trust bring warmth to your spirit!

I am the Way
(John 14: 6)

My child, the important aspects of My love are endless!

In just one human life, these aspects include:

> The shielding of My love
> The healing of My love
> The victory of My love (making
>   strong)
> The peace of My love
> The change-bringing influence of
>   My love
> The hope-producing of My love
> The courage-imparting of My love

When My word of love reaches a human heart at a deep level, it always means that further words are not necessary!

My God will meet all your needs according to His glorious riches in Christ Jesus.
(Philippians 4: 19)

*T*he road which leads to knowing Me is the only road upon which My help is given. No other road carries an assurance of a blest future, no matter how many hardships are encountered upon that road.

The intensity of My love of My children is expressed in My desire that not one of them is lost.

I long to ease the burden of those in great suffering, and I lend My strength in order that those upon My road will find that, eventually, their steps will be easier.

Everything you encounter on *My* road, (however temporarily hard) proves infinitely worthwhile.

**Do not let anyone
lead you astray**
(1 John 3: 7)

*I*t is sad that so often a painful episode of life is encountered, before My importance in the life of one of My children is realised.

Yes, My child, the great tragedy of humanity is its *indifference,* when My resources could have made a vital difference.

If it were not for indifference, the whole course of countless lives would have been changed, and the resultant emptiness and heartbreak avoided.

My child, surrounded by so much scepticism and thoughtlessness, never be ashamed of your allegiance to Me, even if, from time to time, the world pities you.

You will not come to Me to have life
(John 5: 40)

My child, in heaven there will be a place, still, for My meeting of need for My faithful ones who now dwell with Me.

There will be a place, still, for you to meet *My* need of your love and loyalty.

While earth continues to be a place so very much under the influence of evil forces, I will still be in sorrow of heart over that earth.

All that My children must cling to is the promise of My eventual victory, even more when desperate need continues.

... Man of Sorrows
(Isaiah 53: 3)

*T*o be aware of your weakness and, at the same time, to contemplate My power over all things... You are never left with a paralysing sense of weakness once you open up yourself to My strengthening presence.

Countless souls who now dwell in the heavenly places, knew an earthly sense of powerlessness which drove them to throw themselves upon the one who, alone, could adequately minister to them.

My child even if the sense of My presence is scarcely discernible in your state of weakness. I can *still* grant an uplifting sense of My companionship.

**When I am weak,
then I am strong**
(2 Corinthians 12: 10)

*I*n My heavenly home you will find so many who blindly responded to My *mercy*...

To give expression to My mercy, I allowed a temporary victory by the forces of darkness in the lives of so many of My children. Evil's victory was allowed *only* to pave the way for My own victory, in which My children could share.

My child, consistently put all your trust in My mercy, which is My love finding its true expression.

All genuine and lasting encounters with Myself on earth are with My *mercy*.

**The Lord your God
is a merciful God**
(Deuteronomy 4: 31)

121

My child, how *little* effort is needed when you really trust Me! In heaven, you will be able simply to rest in My working far more than ever you did upon earth. My work for you, and for all My children, simply go hand in hand. A work in which I delight.

Always be ready for Me to prompt you if you are failing in your trust.

Thank Me for My working in *present* circumstances and thank Me for the certainty of My working for you in that unknown future.

**We are the servants of
the God of heaven and earth**
(Ezra 5: 11)

*T*he decision for Me, as you have found in your earthly life, affects for good all the many decisions to be made before your life comes to an end.

Once your life has been given to Me, many circumstances will be decided for you, without the agony of a major decision. One crucial choice, almost without your thinking about it, is to make your eventual home in heaven!

Let your own prayers always make a space for your request that My children upon earth would live with Me rather their pursuing a life without Me.

Equipping you for all that is good, having chosen His will
(Hebrews 13: 21)

*I*t is possible for a heart to become hardened in many areas without one being conscious of this.

My Kingdom *only* permits the humble and wistful heart of a child, otherwise one could feel out of place among hearts which have been softened by love.

One area where a hardening of the heart can so easily occur is in attitudes towards those struggling children who do not appear to have made the same spiritual progress as oneself.

Yes, My child, there is no room in the heavenly places for spiritual pride.

**If I do not have love,
I am nothing...**
(1 Corinthians 13: 2)

My child, why does My light shine best in dark places, following the pattern of earth?

It is no accident that in the midst of despair and hopelessness when on earth I revealed Myself as the light of the world.

My children will always reach out from the darkness in vain, until they encounter Myself. I then become a guide through the maze of earth's circumstances.

When life grows dark, always look earnestly for Me, because I love to respond to your looking, by shining upon the darkened way.

God... made His light to shine in our hearts... in the face of Christ Jesus
(2 Corinthians 4: 6)

*L*ife with Me has always been prone to great discouragement. Looking at the many apparent imperfections in My creation and the degree of human suffering, even the most fervent follower of Mine may be tempted to feel that he or she has been mistaken in their hope.

At all costs, look nowhere but to Me when discouraged. Resolutely set against the disturbing factors, the *love* of which you are sure, and which has never failed you.

My child, you will find companions in heaven who have chosen, blindly, to go on trusting, when it seemed almost foolish to do so.

Will you also go away?
(John 6: 67)

*T*he one great requirement, involving no undue effort, is to *keep on the heavenly road*, resisting all that you know is not of Me.

You have found that there are so many lures. If followed, there is so often a long and painful road back to the covering of My love.

At all times, visualise the *brightness* of My presence to keep you on the safe road. It is a brightness which evil has never extinguished.

**The way is narrow
which leads to life**
(Matthew 7: 14)

*U*ntil the day that you arrive in heaven you can create a small 'heavenly place' in your everyday life.

Resolutely turning your back on all current anxieties, and throwing yourself upon My love, is the first step. Speaking My name, as I have told you, will always bring the heavenly realm close for you.

If there has been any great disturbance in your spirit, your remaining in the earthly 'heavenly place' will, after a while begin to restore you.

My yoke is easy
(Matthew 11: 30)

*T*he only real effort which a Christian upon earth is called upon to make, is to keep Me absolutely central to one's existence.

My day-to-day promptings, reminders of My presence, are designed to help you in keeping Me in first place in your heart.

Responding to My promptings will save you from wasteful effort in life's varied fortunes.

If I can establish you on the heavenly road in face of earthly complexities, it is all that matters!

The Name which is above every name
(Philippians 2: 9)

$\mathcal{M}$y child, the sheer precious quality of what I give to you is never diminished by your spiritual weariness or lack of physical well-being.

It so often happens that a blessing is received when a child of Mine summons up an effort to turn in My direction against the pressure of circumstances.

To a sense of My love is added My gift of healing at a deep level. This is why any temporary disinclination to seek Me robs you of so much!

...turn their eyes to the Holy One
(Isaiah 17: 7)

*T*he heavenly places are free of all impurities.

The environment is completely without anything discordant in order that all will harmonise for the pure soul who has been made ready to live in My near presence.

The environment is one which assists the very highest of human aspirations and one which produces contentment of a kind never experienced on earth.

Create in Me a pure heart, O God
(Psalm 51: 10)

Y ou must not be surprised if the events of earth threaten to take away your belief in Me.

Resolutely cling to Me at such times, knowing that as you express your trust and your gratitude, *faith will always return.*

Visualise My going ahead of you through the world's darkness, as I lead to the realm of light, which is your destiny.

My child, your original choice of Myself means that faith is never completely lost.

Simon, pray that your faith may not fail...
(Luke 22: 32)

*N*ever be tempted to give yourself to any worldly manifestation (however plausible) in which I am left out.

It is my presence which adds immeasurably to the gifts of earth.

Make it a discipline to thank Me when enjoying earth's gifts of music, nature's beauty, all that has the touch of innocence, and is free from conflict.

Think on these things...
(Philippians 4: 8)

My child, mere intellect will always fail you if you try to find a rational explanation of My creation.

In its present state, it is a 'fallen' creation with many imperfections of which you are aware... a fallen creation because of the original rebellion of evil forces to spoil My love's design.

But be encouraged, My child; the heavenly is the all-important part of existence, and is *guarded*, as I have told you. Therefore, nothing can keep you from My love, if that is your desire.

Great is your love, O Lord, reaching to the heavens
(Psalm 57: 10)

$\mathcal{B}$ecause an effort is so often needed to follow what you know to be a right course, there is the greatest temptation to compromise with the truth in your heart and to go even slightly astray.

In My realm, the presence of love brings about a natural obedience. This is shown in giving oneself to the heavenly ministry... with the reward of seeing what was almost lost being claimed for Myself.

A human soul brought out of darkness to light, through your agency, is your *present* to Me, as was the gift of your own heart!

Do everything in love...
(1 Corinthians 16: 14)

I want you to go *through* the clouds which encompass you upon earth. Yes, they are daunting, but if you deliberately allow your heavenly Companion to go with you, you will find that you had no need to dread those clouds.

My companionship is to ensure that the dangers of the earthly existence can never harm you. However dark the clouds, the light is never completely obscured.

The light of My presence is no more than a glimpse of heaven in the threatening clouds but it will always be sufficient if you steadfastly follow it.

**The Lord turns my
darkness into light**
(2 Samuel 22: 29)

*I*n any fear of the unknown, there always lurks an element of fear of divine judgement.

My child, if you have made Me your hope, even in the midst of many failures, My justice is tempered by what I have so often stressed to you as My principal attribute... My mercy.

It is the *welcoming* nature of My mercy which makes it easier to turn from wrong aspects within you.

In the realm of heaven, I wish you to keep the sense of gratitude for all that I have come to mean to you... above all, of course, My never-failing mercy.

The Lord our God is merciful
(Daniel 9: 9)

My child, think much of *My* pleasure, added to yours, on your arrival at your heavenly home.

I have watched all your struggles and trials upon earth and have been profoundly comforted by all your efforts to trust Me and to tread My revealed ways. Hence, My joy when you eventually complete your journey.

At heaven's entrance, it will indeed be the greeting of a Friend for you... Myself!

For you it will be a completely new and rewarding environment. Your delight, *My* delight.

...He will take great delight in you
(Zephaniah 3: 17)

*H*eaven waits. My promised consummation of all things in existence is eagerly awaited by the throngs of My saved children. In the hearts of those children is the vision of My light banishing all evil designs, all sadness, all imperfection. Many of those children in the heavenly realm will have played a part in preparation for My coming in glory, by helping to relieve mankind's suffering. They themselves will have tasted suffering, and been led to express the love and empathy developed in them.

My child, look forward to the companionship of those who wait eagerly!

Blessed are all who wait for Him!
(Isaiah 30: 18)

*T*he constant search for Myself
through all the complexities of
existence...

Yes, it is so often an agonising
search, because so much conspires
to obscure Me.

But be re-assured, My child, that
the search for Me never proves,
ultimately, to have been in vain.
The reward of diligent seeking is
My granting true peace of heart.

In the heavenly Kingdom the search
comes to an end for it is there that I
am manifested in a way which
allows of no doubting.

My child, be sure that you never tire
of looking for Me and opening your
heart ever more widely to Me.

**If with all your heart you seek
for Me, you will find Me**
(Jeremiah 29: 13)

I made clear when on earth that there were ways of mankind which made difficult the attainment of heaven. Above all, I revealed My sadness, always, at finding *the unloving heart.*

I revealed My sadness at finding the pride which crushed the spirits of My struggling ones... children whom I would dearly have wished to find comfort in My arms. Although the secrets of the human heart are so often hidden from the world around, I always see through to the *coldness* which betrays the presence of evil.

My child, never let life's circumstances, however daunting, take from your heart the sense My own love; this ensures a divine *warmth* being received by those you meet upon the way.

The love of most will grow cold
(Matthew 24: 12)

Only with Me can a wrong journey be discontinued before it is too late.

A wrong road taken at an early stage in life will carry increasingly harmful consequences and, without Me, be almost impossible to leave.

If I am sought, with a heartfelt desire to turn from the prison of a disastrous road, My mercy is always there to save... a rescue which is both instant and thorough.

My child, heaven is populated by many who made that desperate turning while there was time!

**Today you will be
with Me in paradise**
(Luke 23: 43)

*A*lways be very vigorous in refusing to act upon a lie! There is a constant temptation to stifle the voice of conscience if advantage may be gained.

Yes, My child, *everything* of Me is of truth. Even when what I tell you may (for the moment) be hard to understand, you can be sure that the truth of what I have told you *will* be made clear by events.

You can never stray from My path if you earnestly welcome only what is true... truths anchored deep within your heart.

The sense of My peace will always accompany that awareness that you have followed truth.

**For this I came into the world...
to testify to the truth**
(John 18: 37)

*T*he creator of all things becomes, above all, a *Friend* for a child who wishes to find the way to heaven.

The Friend takes your hand to gently guide you, if you wish no other than to possess Me. Always value that possession of Myself; all else, as you know, is passing and empty.

The road may often seem daunting when you first set out upon it but in the company of your Friend it is infinitely more sure than any other road through life.

A Friend leading along a *planned* way...
A Friend there for you at its end...

The Lord will guide you always
(Isaiah 58: 11)

*E*arthly things which appear to cause others no distress, but cause *you* pain... My child this is yet another indication that earth is not your home!

As you have found, so much on the worldly scene is shallow, and I have given you the insight not to be swept away by such things.

A world in which there is so much darkness and apparent futility can be almost heartbreaking for a sensitive child of Mine, but that very world can be the setting for the quieter gifts of the heavenly.

If you are constantly aware of how I am using earthly phenomena to further My eternal purposes, it will bring you many blessings, blessings which others may never experience.

You do not belong to the world
(John 15: 19)

*M*y child, catch a glimpse of what all things are moving towards.

In spite of the fiercest-possible opposition, there is an inevitable and unstoppable movement to *wholeness* in creation's many aspects.

Heaven represents the culmination of the very highest of human aspirations. It is here that a soul finds real hope, at last, in the one place where such hope can flower.

Yes, in preparation for that one true place of hope, evil will be utterly crushed.

Love's victory!

It is accomplished
(John 19: 30)

You can only endure a world of imperfection and great darkness by the sure hope of My heaven.

My child, heaven is built upon experience of worldly pain. As you endure such pain, I develop in you a readiness to enter a totally new and bright existence.

Yes, after earth's struggles, heaven is supremely the place of contrast. It is here that My love can finally see sorrow turned to joy for a child whom I have watched over.

The state of heaven proclaims My final victory... a victory always planned with My children in My mind.

The Lord will fulfil His purposes
(Psalm 138: 8)

Once you have been placed by Myself upon the heavenward road, it is never long before I take you out of those periods of despair so that you may go forward.

Although the way can be wearisome, the fact that you are Mine means that a sense of hope simply *must* break through.

It is the hope originating in Me that gives you what otherwise you would lack... a resolve and a reliance upon My strength.

The world will marvel when it sees a child whom I have lifted from despair acting with a grace which may not have seemed natural to that child.

The Lord lifts up those who are bowed down
(Psalm 146: 8)

*T*he *faithfulness* of one of My children is the one virtue, above all, which touches My heart.

Life's circumstances are largely out of your control, and for the most part, it is a question of leaning upon Me and sharing those circumstances with Me.

Although your trust in Me so often wavers, I look beyond this and see the faithful heart... the heart which always returns to Me.

Such faithfulness on your part is a response to My own towards you.

My child, what I see *now* is what you are becoming. Therefore, never cease to look forward.

**Your faithfulness, O Lord,
continues through all generations**
(Psalm 119: 90)

*M*y child you have realised that your brief existence upon earth would never be sufficient for the working out of My greater purposes. Earthly existence is an interlude of a very painful nature for so many, simply because much is not yet redeemed.

Let it comfort you that the period in which you inhabit the world is only of minor importance in the divine plan, even though, to you, it seems to fill all things.

Yes, the world sees just a partial reflection of the cosmic struggle against evil forces... forces which have been under sentence of defeat following My earthly victory.

**The plans of the Lord
stand firm for ever**
(Psalm 33: 11)

*N*o-one can ever force their way into heaven!

A child whose steady desire has been to be with Me one day will find that I gently open heaven's gates and *lift* that child into that new sphere.

It is love which greets those who enter... a love which can be overwhelming where, on earth, there has been only experience of hatred or of loneliness.

My child, if earth's experiences have been bitter, never let go of the truth that there exists a love which is able to erase and heal all the pain.

The Lamb in the midst of the throne will be their shepherd
(Revelation 7: 17)

$\mathcal{Y}$ou have experienced how life so often throws one into the unfamiliar, no matter how cautious one tries to be.

Are you grateful, My child, that there is a source of what is familiar and re-assuring to which you can always turn? Yes, there is, *in My Person* the only completely unchanging and secure place in the whole of existence.

When you turn to Me, it is coming to the Rock in the waters of instability. When you reach out to Me it is acknowledging the very precious fact that I am with you at every moment; that I will be *your* ever-present Friend.

**I am the Lord your God,
your Saviour**
(Isaiah 43:3)

γou have touched the heavenly realm simply by keeping close to Me but because of the nature of the material world, My presence may not be accompanied by pure joy at all times!

Pure joy will be yours, one day, My child, as the natural consequence of *seeing Me as I am*. Even in an imperfect world, My presence can mean more and more to you as you persevere in following My way.

When your present existence is left behind, there will open out an entirely new dimension where you need never strive to experience happiness; you will simply feed upon that which My love brings.

**Being with You,
I desire nothing else...**
(Psalm 73: 25)

$\mathcal{M}$y child, have you paused to notice the deeper significance of the little acts which you carry out to please Me? What you do at such times is allowing Me to *prepare* you for life in My Kingdom.

Your acts of love and obedience are never lost, even if you, for the moment, forget them; they have built up your state of being made ready.

Not only are those acts of love a preparation for heaven; your faithfulness towards Me at times of suffering is also a preparation.

To know that I am preparing you for that far better place will always steady you when life is threatening.

Your life is hidden in Christ
(Colossians 3: 3)

*T*here is nothing more tragic than when a child of earth tries to go through life without Me, dismissing even the thought of Me. Such a child should know that that in the perspective of eternity, a life which has My involvement is fulfilling a vital part in My plans for creation, even if that life knows much suffering.

A life shared with Me is able to contemplate the truths which I reveal, and is always forward-looking; it is a life which cannot be other than enriched by My sharing.

My child, can you see why you must value our relationship at all costs?

Life more abundant...
(John 10: 10)

$\mathcal{M}$y child, there will always be things upon which you have set your heart, either for yourself or for others...

I want you not to fret about those times when what you desire is delayed by the world's chances. Remember that anything which gives further opportunity for My working can only be right. Try to see delay in that light, and it will give you patience.

I am constantly at work to make every aspect of your life come into harmony with My purposes for you, and will always give you *just sufficient* courage to hold on to My working.

Let patience have its perfect work
(James 1: 4)

My child, there is one thing above all others which threatens your eventual entry into heaven.

The danger is always the deliberate stifling of My gentle prompting... a self-will which has not died.

You are right to trust My mercy extravagantly (almost foolishly, some will think!) but when you purposefully put aside My whisper in your heart (even temporarily), the path I have planned for you is made more difficult.

Evil is always present, in any self-will, to thwart My designs.

**The road is broad
which leads to destruction**
(Matthew 7: 13)

You have found that if you try to follow Me, the quality of *endurance* will always be needed, above all.

In those times when life becomes very dark and you can see no way out, there is the strongest temptation even to give up your walk with Me, but I know that you will not yield to it.

When tempted to abandon a life of trust, never surrender the thought of what one day awaits you. Firmly keep that thought before you.

Heaven is no mere source of false comfort; it is the one sure fact of existence, and the birthright of every trusting child.

Yes, My child, *your* birthright...

**Be of good courage;
I have overcome the world**
(John 16: 33)

*W*ith so much at stake in the vastness of creation, you will often be made aware of the subtlety and ruthlessness of evil. Although you dare not fail to recognise these forces at work, I wish you never to fear what evil can do to a shielded child, as you are. Although severely tested, never destroyed.

My child, contemplate, often, the demonstration of My love at the Cross; it was there that the powers of darkness incited human hearts to hate all that I stood for, and to destroy Me as the true earthly revelation of the Godhead.

If you cling to Me, My love will always bring victory for you, as it did at the time of My sacrifice.

Thanks be to God who gives us victory through our Lord Jesus Christ
(1 Corinthians 15: 57)

$\mathcal{M}$y child, on your earthly pilgrimage it is important that you recognise what is of Me, to know what are My pure promptings...

The prompting to lift another's load without any lurking self-motivation, *is of Me.*

The prompting to abandon resentment and make peace even when feeling you had been clearly wronged, *is of Me.*

The prompting to ignore, completely, your despondency and to reach out with a word of encouragement, *is of Me.*

The spontaneous and surprising re-kindling of hope in your heart after touching the depths of despair, *is of Me.* All is part of My light banishing the world's darkness!

That you may be children of light
(John 12: 36)

My child, consider your heavenly citizenship!

You can recognise that citizenship by your feeling never quite 'at home' in the material world.

Knowing you before you even came into the world, and knowing that you would come to trust Me, I decreed that heaven was to be your home.

Acknowledging the spiritual can be difficult in the natural world, but can you not see that your own instinct always to return to Me is yet another proof that your *true* home is in heaven?

Your heart is where your treasure is
(Matthew 6: 21)

*T*o wish for heaven is never mere selfishness, or in any way unworthy.

Understand that because of My mercy, the failures in your life are put behind Me *if a heavenly desire is present* on your part.

Implicit in your wish to come to be with Me one day is an intention (often unconscious at first), to live according to My will.

The desire for heaven is, of course, met by My own desire! That desire is to usher in a child who realises, at the gate of heaven, that his or her wish was not something self-created after all.

Fix your mind on God's Kingdom
(Matthew 6: 33)

*T*he nature of the earthly existence means that it is possible to lose the way to one's eternal destiny.

When the way is lost, and you are painfully conscious of this, the only sure guidepost is Myself. Only I can plant your feet firmly on the true path again, with My hand holding yours.

If you have earnestly sought Me, after wandering you can be assured that I am leading you safely once more.

Yes, My child, you are not merely trusting One who knows the way, but who *is* the Way. That is why ensuring your closeness to Me - desperately - means that you cannot be lost.

He will not let your foot slip...
(Psalm 121: 3)

$\mathcal{M}$y child, so much of the brightness of My resurrected presence is light from My many victories over the world's darkness.

There has been victory when I was able to draw a lost child back to Myself.

There has been victory whenever bruised relationships on earth were healed.

There has been victory when a child of Mine has used the courage which I give to stand firm and cause evil to retreat.

Never cease to value *love* wherever you find it. So often in the darkest places!

Love is made complete among us
(1 John 4: 17)

*T*he ultimate sadness is when a child who has tried to follow Me comes to feel utter separation from Me. Yes, a sense of separation can come at certain times to even the most dedicated child.

I always feel, acutely, any temporary sense of estrangement which you may have, and that is why I constantly work to restore an awareness of unity with Myself.

My child, whenever you picture My arms of love opened widely for you, you are opening your heart to My working, so that *what is in your mind's eye becomes reality*. Able, once again, to feel rested and secure in Myself.

Who can separate us from the love of Christ?
(Romans 8: 35)

*I*n any very painful situation be very sure that you have, *with your whole heart*, given that situation to Me.

Where there has been that complete surrender to Myself I want you to trust that whatever then comes about is *of Me*... Always see *My* hand in the events which I allow however puzzling or distressing they may be.

Steadfastly think of My faithful love at such times and, of course, tell Me that you trust that love.

You have come to realise that in My heart is the unchanging intention to bring about what I see is best for you; therefore trust Me with every fibre of your being, and let nothing quench your spirits.

...to understand how incredibly great is His power to help those who believe in Him
(Ephesians 1: 19)

*Y*ou cannot see the hand which reaches out towards you so frequently at times of great need. The hand outstretched is to mark My close *identification* with you.

When I touched the needy people whom I encountered on earth, it was a mark of that same identification. The reaching-out takes our relationship beyond mere theory, to show that I am never unmoved by your need.

My child, always welcome the outstretched divine hand, and think of it often. That same hand will take yours one day not merely to carry you through temporary crises but especially to establish you in heaven.

What do you want Me to do for you?
(Luke 18: 41)

$\mathcal{M}$y child, is there an *intensity* about your longing for heaven?

Life with Me always demands that there are no half-measures; to value Me must be placed above all else and expressing Me in your world must be your principal concern.

It is a question of *giving everything* to knowing Me and My ways. Your pattern is My own giving of Myself for you at a cost you can only imagine.

The world would not have been saved, nor heaven made the hope of My children, if I had not loved to the very limit.

**Let your true satisfaction
be in knowing Me**
(Jeremiah 9: 24)

I have given you My promise
that fear will be unknown in the
heavenly places. That freedom from
fear which so often seems hard to
achieve in an earthly life, is
nevertheless something to which
you can look forward.

Fear can so easily be present by
the very nature of creation's
imperfections, but do not forget the
resources which are yours, My
child...

Whenever you turn to Me you can
expect My love to *minister* to you,
instantaneously, striking at the very
root of fear in your heart. Yes, My
love will wear down the fear, even
if you feel no strength in yourself to
conquer it!

**If I set you free,
you really are free!**
(John 8: 36)

I have a special place in My love for those with tender hearts who have known great sadness... in a busy world, those children are often seen as being of no consequence.

For those whom life has hurt, there will be a place at My side in My Kingdom of light; in a very real sense, they will *possess* that Kingdom!

There will always be a sadness in My own heart. It is these especially-chosen ones, whose privilege it will be to minister to that sadness.

It was truly said of these, My children, that the last shall be first...

The Kingdom of heaven is theirs...
(Matthew 5: 2)

It is the seemingly-small things of life which can bring to you a touch of heaven. These things are brought to you so often, when there is a desperate need of encouragement, when worldly aspects seem completely beyond solution.

Then, into the despair, comes a simple kind act, a word of genuine understanding (often from surprising sources). You can be sure that these things were planned by Me for your need as I saw it, often without the human agent being aware of the divine purpose.

My child, if a kindness which speaks of heaven touches your heart, be assured that there will be *many more* such tokens!

Led beside water-springs...
(John 4: 18)

My child, when do you appreciate My love most?

Is it not at those times when you feel that such love has not been 'deserved' in the worldly sense?

It is only when My love shines through in spite of your failures that *true* gratitude can be felt.

Do not be afraid to face with Me, those things in your life about which you feel ashamed (often half-forgotten). As you do this, you may see no good reason why I should love you as I do. This My child, is the beginning of true humility and My love will *still* come to overwhelm you!

**His goodness and mercy
will follow me all my life**
(Psalm 23: 6)

γou have often found yourself unable to do or to say anything apart from leaving a matter entirely in My hands!

As you realise, these are times of learning My faithfulness... something which you may not have learned to the full when you were able to influence events yourself.

My child, I never allow your power-lessness in a situation to prevent My bringing about what I see is right for you.

So often, on looking back, you find that you have cause to thank Me for those times when you were completely unable to control events yourself. Things were 'made right' for you. Frequently in way you could not have predicted!

With God, all things are possible...
(Mark 10: 27)

*I*n the heavenly Kingdom, My children will be set free from the need, in any way, to strive.

On earth, a trusting child soon learns that I can wonderfully bless even the smallest effort committed to Me.

When heaven is reached, effort will not be needed to carry out My law of pure love, because My children will be carried in ways of expressing love as a perfectly natural thing. *My* influence will be in those acts of love!

My child, as I have told you, effortless obedience will simply flow from full surrender to Me.

Be strong in the Lord
(Ephesians 6: 10)

My child, never accept anything less than the fact that *all is subject to Me.*

You will need to keep this in your mind whenever you find yourself in circumstances which you believe I brought about, and yet are unable to see the reasons for the place you are at!

Yes, I have to teach My children what it is to be completely thrown back upon Me, conscious only of one's own helplessness, but trusting that I will in some way carry you through that unknown future.

Whenever you are puzzled by the events allowed in your life, what is important is your determination to go into that unknown future *with Me.*

Able to do immeasurably more than we can ask or imagine
(Ephesians 3: 20)

My child, the world will dismiss as wishful thinking the vision in many human hearts of a place of joy and freedom.

Far from wishful thinking, the vision of heaven is based on a deep instinct that what I have made known is true.

Love cannot die, nor can My eternal reign be lost. The future of My created children is so much in the divine mind.

Never feel even slightly unsure as you contemplate what I have revealed of My heavenly Kingdom. Be assured that upon earth truth will *always* triumph in the end, foreshadowing the triumph of love in My creation as a whole.

An inheritance incorruptible
(1 Peter 1: 4)

*N*ever disbelieve that very quiet re-assurance which suddenly comes into your heart at a time of darkness; it is a re-assurance that beyond earthly phenomena all is well.

My child, never be moved from this comforting belief. Look up to Me from periods of suffering, and express a word of gratitude that there *is* a far better place to satisfy the human spirit.

My resurrection was a revelation that the *real* victory is always with love and truth. My child, ponder that resurrection and the way in which it transformed the sorrow of the privileged few of My followers.

Just as My triumph will eventually transform all darkness...

God's eternal purpose accomplished in Christ Jesus
(Ephesians 3: 17)

*J*ust as heaven is My domain, where My authority is exerted, so too the material world is subject to My rule. The earthly rule, though not always apparent, is demonstrated by the frequent times that evil's designs are brought to nothing and My children are saved from what would be disastrous for their future.

So much of My earthly rule is on a scale beyond your immediate knowledge, but it is always exerted in order that love may triumph, even when the forces of darkness seem to enjoy the ascendancy.

My child, the divine rule is seen *beyond all question* in heaven, unlike the clouding of earth. Look forward to enjoying My lordship in heaven, with evil finally and utterly defeated.

The Lord Jesus Christ - the same yesterday, today and for ever
(Hebrews 13: 8)

My children long for My interventions... wishing that these would be more frequent. Yes, this has always been mankind's *heartfelt* cry... that the divine power would be manifest when wickedness and innocent suffering were so prevalent.

Understand that I have always intervened in the lives of My children imprisoned by the circumstances of a material creation.

I have reached out to My children with the knowledge (possessed only by Myself) of their future and the need to preserve their free will. These interventions have occurred when it was vital that a child should be saved from forces threatening destruction at that time. My child, be sure that I have so often stepped into *your* life's circumstances.

He restores my soul
(Psalm 23: 3)

*U*nderstand, My child, that the many dwelling places of heaven are in a state of preparation for those souls, as yet unsaved, whom I will draw to Myself. Those souls, at present lost, are already known to Me, as you yourself have always been.

No matter what man may conjecture of My purposes, the very nature of My love is that I *do not wish any human soul to be ultimately lost.*

As I said when on earth, I always pursue, as the Good Shepherd, those who, in various ways, have wandered.

Only infinite love could eventually gather even the most hardened souls to My heart.

**There are other sheep
who will listen to My voice**
(John 10: 16)

Only those rescued by Me from far wandering could know the full meaning of My searching for the lost. Only those who were found by Myself could fully enter into the homecoming joy of the heavenly places.

My child, your companions in the angelic ministry will so often be those who were rescued, even when all hope for them seemed to have been abandoned.

Until the end of time My children will be called to be angels, having a consciousness within them of the infinitude of the divine love which brought them to their true home.

**Today you will be with
me in paradise**
(Luke 22:23)

*T*he darkness which I allow in My creation has a decided purpose... that purpose is that My children should know something of the poignancy of the eternal struggle with the enemies of love and human happiness.

After My children have experienced, on earth just a little of the eternal conflict, I can open for them, after life's trials, an existence where, at last, the unfailing truth of hope is clearly seen.

Yes, what will be learned by My children is the *vulnerability* of love... a vulnerability which, in spite of its apparent weakness, carries in itself the seeds of final victory.

Our momentary light afflictions are achieving for us an eternal glory that far outweighs them all
(2 Corinthians 4: 17)

*T*o see with *My* eye is always to be aware of the darkness which underlies present existence.

Yes, My child, to know truth can be painful where it reveals all that is not of My Kingdom of light, where it reveals what is shallow or even false.

The pain felt by a sensitive soul can, however, serve a good purpose if it drives one to embrace desperately, only what is worthy in the worldly existence.

It is only as you deliberately place yourself in the refuge provided in such a world that you can see everything outside My presence as of no lasting consequence...

**Whoever follows truth
will walk in the light**
(John 3: 21)

*I*t is good to think of heaven at any stage of the earthly life, not merely when nearing life's end. It is the thought of heaven which gives meaning to one's existence in the world.

To have heaven in one's thoughts as a permanent thing, saves one from many pitfalls; it saves one from action due to expediency. Above all, the thought of heaven gives the much-needed sense of proportion to the medley of experiences, good and bad, in which one finds oneself.

Not only will the thought of a future existence prompt to many good deeds which may never have been attempted but it will mean a restraining hand on what would be dangerously unwise!

Let this mind be in you which was in Christ Jesus
(Philippians 2: 5)

*T*here has to be an element of mystery about the heavenly realm. Fleeting glimpses of heaven come to make endurable the earthly existence, but much has to be closed to your present knowledge.

The one *certain* experience of the heavenly for My children upon earth is to know my presence. When you reach heaven, having faithfully kept upon My road, you will look back to realise how I sustained you.

My child, what is in store for you is far more than a passive role in My Kingdom. As well as gaining new knowledge, you will share My active ministry, which is endless.

Now we see but a poor reflection in a mirror, but then we shall see face to face
(1 Corinthians 13: 12)

*I*t is often felt by those who do not fully understand My ways that My mercy may be too indulgent and that I make it too easy for a return to Me after wandering into ways which have hurt Me, about which there was true sorrow.

My child, understand why I lovingly lift you out of the place where your wandering left you. It is simply that at no time do I wish to lose you.

If I did not provide a way back to Me and you were confronted only by My justice, you would feel that relations between us could never be restored.

Remember that when I was on earth, it was My love which rescued many who were going astray. My child, ponder this deeply.

**No one can take My children
out of My hand**
(John 10: 28)

My child, on the road to heaven
in the midst of a world of struggle
you will find that I give you
travelling companions.

You will know by what you receive
in hope and courage from those
who join you on the road that they
were sent to you by Myself.

Sometimes those I provide for you
will be for virtually your life's
entire journey. Pray that you will
recognise them. Others will be
more fleeting companions but
nevertheless sent for the needs of
that moment. Pray that you will
recognise them, also.

So often you will find, on a difficult
road, that you are aware of having a
divine friend *and* a human friend!

The Lord will provide
(Genesis 22: 14)

*T*here is one divine imperative for those wishing to follow Me. Lovingly I make known to you what I always require of you: *look nowhere but to Me.*

As you bring back to Me all wandering thoughts and impulses, frequently speaking My name, you are walking upon the very narrow way leading to life. Looking nowhere but to Me, you are hidden in Me, more and more, with fewer and fewer intrusions into our precious relationship.

Looking nowhere but to Me, I am bringing you through all the present trials in your life as only I can. My child, I will always strengthen you if your desire is to look only to Me.

If you follow Me, you will not walk in darkness
(John 8: 12)

*D*oubt of heaven is of the same area as doubt of Me.

Doubt about there being any other existence than the material can easily come upon contemplation of a fallen world.

Yes, a fallen world with all its seemingly-random suffering, its injustices and the deep-seated darkness so often seen in man.

My child, it is because I was in that fallen world, and subject to its very worst aspects that I long for the redemption of all human souls.

My purpose is the reign of love not only in heaven , but eventually in the very darkest places of earth.

**The whole creation groans,
right up to the present time**
(Romans 8: 22)

$\mathcal{M}$ere thought can never make one sure of heaven!

The truth of heaven does not lend itself to the way of reasoning based on the phenomena you can observe.

You have become sure of heaven, My child, by getting to know Me, because this *knowledge of Myself* makes the human soul aware of the innate goodness at the heart of creation.

Heaven becomes a real hope by the miracle of love existing amid so much that seems without meaning.

Each time My love rescues you from life's darker aspects, your instinctive belief in a future realm of peace is deepened.

...Peter said... 'Lord you have the words of eternal life'
(John 6: 68)

*Y*ou cannot always know what is true amid the deceptions which have infiltrated My creation.

The only sure way to recognise truth is to observe every matter through the light of Myself; if you discipline yourself to do this - especially in matters where there is doubt - I will not fail to enlighten you.

Where My presence is sought, it will always show you, beyond argument, that something is not of Me and therefore not to be trusted.

You are always safe to trust yourself to any matter where the sense of My *love* is not obscured and there is a witness to that love within your own heart.

...full of grace and truth
(John 1: 14)

*T*here are many places where the road to heaven has to be steep. Because of the prize that awaits, I have to see a child's perseverance and unchanging desire for Myself.

My child, the road taken with Me will never be more difficult than you can bear; I allow precisely what is right in life's circumstances to test your endurance, but without pain.

Along the steep places keep in your mind that heaven is your goal. There may be no human assistance in those places but there will be an unseen presence (My own) drawing you upwards.

See adversity as one of the steeper places and always let such adversity be transformed by the thought of what awaits you at the road's end.

Lead Me in a straight path
(Psalm 27: 11)

My child, I have repeatedly urged you to ensure that My love dwells in you; this is because so much is achieved by my love *alone*. Therefore let love encompass everything.

The power of love is such that it overcomes worldly force; love's power is such that it changes hearts more than argument could ever do.

If you hide in My love at all times you are *made* courageous and victorious over despair in surprising ways.

In spite of enticements for your thoughts to wander, look consistently towards Me. As you look into My countenance, so much is automatically undertaken on your behalf.

If I do not have love, I am nothing
(1 Corinthians 13: 3)

What awaits a child on the very first entry into heaven is simply *sheer kindness*.

So many souls have been hurt on the earthly journey and their first need, even more than seeing My Kingdom's brightness, is to find the tender understanding which may have been absent on earth.

Yes, My child, My kingdom is built on many good acts through the centuries, and that is why kindness and compassion shine out through that kingdom.

As I have told you, the secret of the entire often-mysterious creation is simply love. Heaven is My permanent reflection of that love.

**Jesus showed them the
full extent of His love**
(John 13: 1)

When on earth, I taught My disciples about those who not only experienced heaven, but who had made it their own ('the kingdom... is theirs.')

You have discerned that while in the world, heavenly rewards may never come for those who patiently endure suffering; those rewards kept for heaven.

The heartbroken, the cruelly-treated, the pathetically-deprived, those who have longed for love but never found it, those who long for inner-righteousness, those who make peace...

Not only can these children expect a heavenly reward, but will surely have the joy of sharing *possession* of the Kingdom with Myself!

If we endure, we will also *reign* with Him
(2 Timothy 2: 12)

When a storm rages in your life there is only one place to go... *love's harbour.*

As you place yourself firmly in My love, you can face even the most fearsome of circumstances. All effort of your own to stand up to the storm becomes unnecessary as I shield you.

In the refuge of calm, your own fear will subside, so that you can see your situation, however complex, with greater clarity and tranquillity.

My child, you will, of course, realise that you find, in love's harbour, the peace of heaven!

His banner over me is love
(Song of Songs 2: 4)

My child, if I am your possession *you must not envy!*

What can the world offer that comes near to the precious knowledge of Myself? All that you may envy is passing. Remember this whenever discontent causes you to be troubled in spirit.

When you are tempted to compare your situation with the fortunes of others, turn away from what is evil's lying activity, and in the simplest possible way tell Me, 'Lord, thank You that I have You... the most precious gift'.

As others see how much I mean to you (even when you are brought low by circumstances) they, too, will begin to see how important My presence must be for their own lives.

Godliness, with contentment, is great gain
(1 Timothy 6: 6)

*J*ust as My love pours out to My children in many different ways, so you, too, My child, must allow your knowledge of My love and how much you value Me, to be the source of what flows out from you into the various aspects of life in the world.

All your relationships, all your ambitions, must be affected, in some way, by My love at the centre of your being.

My child, spend a few moments when life is difficult to reflect upon how My love for you will never change. If love is given pride of place in this way it will always be followed by My sure working, based on your present need.

Yes, look into the countenance of My love!

Faith expressing itself through love
(Galatians 5: 6)

*O*nce a warm and wholehearted decision to follow Me has been made, heaven is immediately in prospect, even though there may be many subsequent fallings-back and personal disappointment with one's spiritual state.

The prospect of heaven will always hold good if a child shows the desire, after failure, to re-join the heavenly path.

My child, you can see that *desire* is the vital thing in life with Me. Desire transcending the fluctuations of circumstances and even one's own intermittent attempts to obey My will.

If desire for Me is ever lost, that is always a great sadness. Nurture that desire constantly even when life brings great discouragement.

May He give you the desire of your heart
(Psalm 20: 4)

*M*y child, realise that the divine activity embraces spheres of existence which are closed to your present knowledge.

You would be overwhelmed if you knew how the forces of the universe (frequently expressed in the *angelic* realm), are there to help you on your heavenward journey.

The journey with Me is the only walk of life where there is something ahead for you both to learn and to enjoy.

No road other than Mine offers the peace which proves elusive for so many.

What is unseen is eternal
(2 Corinthians 4: 18)

*H*eaven's enfolding... The whole of creation is encompassed by the heavenly sphere, and yet how close is that sphere to the soul which reaches out to Myself as heaven's embodiment.

The enfolding characteristic of the heavenly places is reflected in the shielding which is granted to who-ever comes to put their trust in Me.

My child, you have long realised that you cannot know the full magnitude of the creation which I rule, nor of the influence of love which contains and safeguards it.

Whenever you think of My love and praise Me for it, you are, for that moment, piercing through the great mystery of My universe.

Chosen in Christ Jesus before the creation of the world
((Ephesians 1: 4))

*T*he many ills which afflict mankind will find an immediate remedy on entering heaven.

Those things which brought struggle and great sadness upon earth (often for a lifetime) will receive the touch of My love. Enlightenment about My plans for the human race will be learned at My feet.

With all the hurt of earth now left behind, My children will find something which could never have been experienced in the days of struggle... an eagerness to learn of My love's plan for mankind, and an eagerness to be part of it.

Yes, My child, the angelic ministry...

I will heal My people and let them enjoy abundant peace
(Jeremiah 33: 6)

A little of the blue of heaven comes to relieve earth's greyness *only* when I am eagerly received into a heart, or into that heart's circumstances.

My child, making room for Myself must always be wholehearted, even when there seems very little strength left to invite Me, after many discouragements.

A child who reaches out to Me with wholeheartedness (often through tears), is showing a desire which always touches My heart.

The touch of heaven which comes to you when room is made for Me, is a foretaste of the glory which will be yours to share with Me.

...so that you may be overjoyed when His glory is revealed
(1 Peter 4: 13)

My child, you have observed
that earth is essentially an
unfinished and tainted environment.
But it is, in spite of this, a place in
which My kingdom is slowly and
painfully built.

One day, My kingdom will envelop
all, in a way which My children will
see very plainly.

Until that time, value the privilege
of seeing the deeds of patience,
courage, and tender love being
used to help the building of that
kingdom.

All these are manifestations of My
Spirit's working in human hearts.
In eternity, not one of these will be
lost.

**The kingdoms of the world have
become the Kingdom of our Lord!**
(Revelation 11: 13)

*O*n your spiritual journey there will often be loneliness.

The often sad moments , when all that you have is Myself are ordained for your deeper experience. Yes, there are opportunities there for you in the solitary places. If you offer those places to Me, I will never fail to use them for your good.

Above all, you will grow in the realisation that My love is all that matters. You will see all your concerns in My light, perhaps for the very first time. Lonely but encouraged!

to grow in the grace and knowledge of our Lord and Saviour...
(2 Peter 3: 18)

*A*t all costs, cultivate that *longing* for heaven...

As one who has committed your life to Me, you can be sure of that longing being fulfilled. Yes, heaven is your destiny.

The chances and bitter disappointments of the material world will so often produce that longing in your heart - a longing for the realm of love and peace.

The thought of heaven is no idle dream; it is the logical expectation of the wonderful promise by Him whom you have come to trust being realised.

**We have this hope
as an anchor**
(Hebrews 6: 19)

My child, do not miss the occasions when heaven breaks through!

Let there be a glad recognition of *My* hand whenever you receive human understanding and help (either expected or unexpected).

Learn to see Me *watching over you* ready to take the opportunity to minister to you, both directly and through others.

Just as My providential care is continuous, so too, there can be a thankfulness on your part which is increasingly unbroken.

He will watch over your life
(Psalm 121: 7)

*A*long the earthly journey, all loving meetings (often chance meetings), pave the way to My eternal home. The many encounters where love is absent serve no purpose.

Any time spent with another child of Mine where you feel the touch of helpfulness and peace brings you an intimation (though imperfect), of the realm where love is all.

Every environment where you do not have to strive, any environment where you can express truth and your deepest feeling without rebuke is a token of the *restfulness* of heaven.

**...being rooted and
established in love**
(Ephesians 3: 17)

My child, My desire was always to have with Me, on My returning to heaven from your earth, a company of saved children to be objects of My love.

These are children who praise Me with hearts which are overflowing with gratitude as they contemplate the darkness and the futility out of which I brought them.

In their hearts I have planted the desire to be My instruments in My cause upon earth. Theirs is both a service, therefore, of praise, and of love for Myself and My children.

Their angels in heaven always see the face of My Father
(Matthew 18: 10)

*B*e constantly receptive to the *intimations of heaven*; see them as coming to you from My hand, as you look to Me. Looking steadfastly to Me, heaven has touched you in these ways...

When a peace suddenly descends on you in a jarring environment...

When you begin to hope again after a period of facing only darkness...

When you feel a confidence which once deserted you, and you can now bravely face the world again...

Yes, My child, I constantly seek opportunities to bring the heavenly into earth's complexities.

**The Lord God will
give them light**
(Revelation 22: 5)

My child, you are growing in the *mind* of heaven when you instinctively cease from striving in a matter and feel, instead, that I have taken the responsibility from you.

The inhabitants of My Kingdom learn an extravagant and child-like acceptance of My very sure working; they learn, gladly, the 'permission to act' on their behalf... which is what I always look for.

The results of this surrender upon earth reflect, in a small way, the perfect carrying-out of My purposes in the wider sphere of My eternity.

...who daily bears our burdens
(Psalm 68: 19)

*I*n heaven there will be a vital difference in the love you are able to feel and to express, compared with earth. Because of the nature of the worldly existence, your capacity to love universally is, to a large extent, restricted.

I will grant to you, in My Kingdom to have a new heart based upon love. You will be able to see *all* My children in the light of My own love.

A heart which can love with no reservations is a heart which I am able to use in the heavenly ministry. My child, I know that you feel very far from that ideal! But My promise is that the highest of all callings will be yours as you give yourself to My love for your remaining days upon earth.

Created in Christ Jesus for good works
(Ephesians 2: 10)

My child, it is My presence which *unites* heaven and earth, and it is in this vital area of My presence that there is no real distinction between the two spheres.

Always try to see heaven as more than a mere continuation of the years upon earth; it is the place where love *reigns*... it is provided for the further development of those to whom My love has come to mean much.

My essential work in the heavenly realm will be to shape souls more and more into My likeness.

I will delight to live in the heavenly places with you, ministering to you. You will have the privilege of giving Me the selfless praise which never reached perfection on earth.

Strengthened in the inner man
(Ephesians 3: 16)

When you contemplate the eventual end of your life upon earth, surrender to Me every moment left to you... for Me to use.

You may never see My using of each moment, but it will bring you great peace to know that I have every future aspect in My hands.

My using of each moment will bring countless instances of being rescued from hazards, great or small, and the future you have placed in My hands will be used to put a golden trust in your heart.

My child, your giving to Me of all the moments still to come will mean a growing gratitude and a growing steadiness.

...able to guard what I have entrusted to Him
(2 Timothy 1: 12)

*M*y child, I give you a small but very important part in My plan for mankind.

The triumph of love in My universe owes more to your simple trust than you could at present imagine.

My creative purposes will always go forward when, in a life such as yours, there is a dependency upon Myself. Your faithfulness and restraint help to ensure that spoilation of My designs by the powers of evil in your life is brought to nothing.

Yes, in spite of temporary opposition, *all* My purposes will be fulfilled.

Be faithful unto death, and I will give you the crown of life
(Revelation 2: 10)

$\mathcal{M}$y child, until your earth is fully redeemed, I will send My angelic messengers to reflect My light in many dark places. it is the same light which will greet the traveller who enters My Kingdom of heaven.

There could be no higher calling than to prepare a fallen world for My eventual coming. It is love which will enter the darkness of many lives, to show up all that I am.

My child, prepare your heart for being a part of this.

Made His light to shine in our hearts
(2 Corinthians 4: 6)

*M*y child, as I have told you,
there will be provision in heaven for
meeting of need.

Even when enjoying the bliss of the
heavenly realm, there will be times
when you feel led to call upon Me.
I will be ready, as I was on earth,
to draw close to you as your Friend
for any need of the spirit to be met.

I am pledged to lovingly stoop
down for a child who feels the need
of My closeness.

Why is this?

My readiness to meet your need is
because My work on behalf of My
children simply cannot cease. My
love must always find fulfilment...
yes, even in the midst of the heavenly!

Your Father knows your need...
(Matthew 6: 8)

*T*o speak of heaven and to utter My name are always best spoken in the same breath! Yes, heaven is simply *My near presence...*

Always remember the unity of the place of wonder, (to which you look forward) with the Saviour whose love sustains it.

When you long for heaven, it is really a longing for Me, a longing for My closeness, a longing to know Me more perfectly. Heaven is simply part of the reward that I represent for you.

Even though you falter, often, My child, My promise stands that nothing can ever take you from Me.

...united with the Vine
(John 15: 4)

My child, I have only been able to tell you a small portion of all the things which make up the heavenly kingdom.

There are many delights, many tranquil periods in which beauty feeds your spirits and many count-less rewarding areas of activity.

Without knowing about these things at present, your preparation for heaven, still, is the very clear one of simply furthering our precious relationship, deepening the bond between us.

Yes, My child, greater-than-ever trust, and greater-than-ever gratitude, even if all you can express gratitude for is that you share life with Me.

...that you might share in the glory of our Lord Jesus Christ
(2 Thessalonians 14)

*Samples from some of
Fr. John's other books are on
the following pages...*

Words taken from 'I Am With You':

I am the hope of all the ends of the earth. But so few truly know it deep in their hearts. In Me lies the fulfilment of the complex desires and possibilities of human nature.

You know that all the qualities you see in Me are available for you. Are you sad, My child, that so often you fail to make use of them? Yes, this is the world's failing - that men do not appropriate that which is there for them, in Me.

Set Me before you always as your one true hope. Be sure that your hand is firmly in Mine ... Proclaim Me as mankind's hope to those around you ... As you recognise the progress you make with Me, so the conviction will grow which you bring to telling others, all that I can be to them!

I know that in your heart is that longing to know Me more perfectly. I honour that longing, and that is why you are sure of My patience in all your failures. It is, of course, My grace which helps you to maintain that longing - and to come, increasingly, into oneness with Myself.

I will never turn away anyone who comes to Me
(John 6: 37)

*T*he reason for My entering the historical process was not merely to reveal My divinity unmistakably.

My incarnation was in order that *love* should become victorious over the many manifestations of evil which spoil the lives of My children.

Underlying My invitation 'Come to Me' was My overall mission to heal the broken-hearted and to release those who are bound in various ways. A mission not to condemn but to save.

As I lift your burdens, think of My joy at seeing that mission of love working in a child's life (yours).

Loved with an everlasting love
(Jeremiah 31: 3)

THE "I AM WITH YOU" FELLOWSHIP

Readers of Fr John's inspired words may join the I Am With You Fellowship. All in the Fellowship are remembered in prayer and are encouraged to write about any particular need. To join, please send your name, address (incl. postcode), phone number and email address (if available) to:

I Am With You Foundation
c/o Good News Books
Upper Level, St John the Apostle Church Complex
296 Sundon Park Road
Luton Beds LU3 3AL
Tel. 01582 571011
email orders@goodnewsbooks.net
www.goodnewsbooks.net

The Foundation distributes mini copies of John Woolley's books free of charge all over the world and relies completely on donations. If you would like to order more minis free of charge or wish to tell us what you feel about the book or want to make a donation in support of this work, please send it to:

I Am With You Foundation
2 Lauradale Road
London N2 9LU, UK
Tel. 020 8883 2665
email: contact@iamwithyou.co.uk

For further information, please visit our website:
www.iamwithyou.co.uk